Strictly Shrimp

Strictly Shrimp

*A Passionate Guide
to the World's
Favorite Seafood*

A. D. LIVINGSTON

BURFORD BOOKS

OTHER BOOKS BY A. D. LIVINGSTON

Strictly Steak: A Passionate Guide to the Great American Feast

Strictly Barbecue: A Passionate Guide to the Right Stuff
(in preparation)

Venison Cookbook

Complete Fish and Game Cookbook

Sausage

Cast-Iron Cooking

On the Grill

Printed in the United States of America

Illustration on page 14 by Sarah Burford

10   9   8   7   6   5   4   3   2   1

Library of Congress Cataloging-in-Publication Data
Livingston, A. D., 1932–
    Strictly shrimp : a passionate guide to the world's favorite seafood /
by A. D. Livingston.
        p.   cm.
    ISBN 1-58080-090-4 (pb.)
    1. Cookery (Shrimp).   2. Shrimps.   I. Title.
TX754.S58 L58   2001
641.6'95—dc21   00-068870

Contents

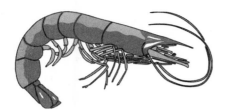

Shrimp Jubilee

A strange thing can happen during a midsummer's night on the eastern shore of Mobile Bay. Shrimp, crabs, and flounder, as well as eels and stingrays and catfish, are compelled to beach themselves, fluttering and scuttling about in the surf. Marine biologists are hard put to set forth a totally satisfactory explanation of the phenomenon in layman's terms, but it's almost certainly caused by a form of oxygen depletion in the water, perhaps in part to decaying organic matter brought into the bay by the nutrient-rich Alabama and Tombigbee Rivers.

Whatever the scientists might say, some of the old salts in the bay area can feel the phenomenon coming days ahead. The air becomes muggy—hot and humid. The wind is out of the east. The water on the east side of the bay is clear and calm, almost like glass. Minnows began to amass on top, as if struggling for air. After two or three days of these conditions, shrimp and other edible bay shellfish and fin fish seem to lose their faculties and begin trying to beach themselves in prodigious numbers.

One explanation points to a culmination of several natural conditions that all come together at no other place in the world; it can be summarized (and surely oversimplified) as a wall of oxygen-deficient water tiding toward the eastern shore. The fish and shellfish try to stay out in front of the wall, but they're pushed closer and closer to the beach until finally they have nowhere to go. This happens always at night (usually after midnight), always in midsummer, and always on rising tide.

A jubilee is not simply a red tide; it's not related to environmental contamination or water pollution; and it doesn't make the fish and shellfish unfit for human consumption. So, as soon as the phenomenon is observed by local fishermen or beach watchers, the cry goes out—

Jubilee! Jubilee!

—and the telephones buzz and the natives grab their flashlights and lanterns and rush by the hundreds to the shore with dip nets and flounder gigs and washtubs for holding the easy bounty. There is good cause to hurry: The jubilee ends as soon as the tide turns or the wind changes, or at the break of day.

Some years will see two or three jubilees in July and August. Other years will have none. The phenomenon was recorded in Mobile newspapers as early as 1876, and records indicate that American Indians took advantage of the event long before the European explorers arrived.

Fortunately, the current residents around Mobile Bay no longer have to rely on a jubilee to get their fill of fresh shrimp and other seafood. Of course, the regulars have always been able to catch a few shrimp for the table, but they were not as plentiful or as easy to catch as you might think. In fact, the *Gulf City Cook Book* (the first American committee-type publication, compiled by the Ladies of the St. Francis Street Methodist Episcopal Church, South Mobile, Alabama, 1878) set forth a whole chapter about the bay oyster but listed only three recipes for shrimp—and one of these called for canned shrimp. Thanks to modern fishing boats, mechanical ice machines, and an insatiable demand from the rest of the country, shrimp are now brought in from deeper waters far out in the Gulf of Mexico as well as inshore. The catch includes white shrimp, brown shrimp, red shrimp, pink shrimp, and others, some with very long whiskers, sometimes compared to a Japanese admiral. Much depends on the season, the salinity of the water, and so on.

This success story from the warm waters of the Gulf of Mexico and along the southeast Atlantic coast can be extended to other parts of the world—including the frigid waters off Maine and Alaska and Scandinavia. As a result, shrimp are now America's favorite shellfish. I read somewhere that New York City alone consumes nearly 2 million pounds of shrimp per week. The annual catch is astounding—several hundred million pounds—and about half the world's market shrimp, including some of the large tiger prawns, are now raised in holding ponds under controlled conditions. Surprisingly, shrimp farming is even taking place in salt ponds in Arizona and other arid places as well as in the rice paddies of India and the mangrove swamps of Singapore. The yield? Count the crop in tons of shrimp per acre, if all goes well.

Truly, now is the time for a shrimp eater's jubilee all over this vast land and around the world. I can only hope that this little book will help spread the word.

—A. D. LIVINGSTON
Wewahitchka, Florida

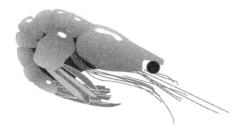

Acknowledgments

I would like to thank the friends, guests, and cooks who have contributed to this book. Specific acknowledgments to individuals, other books, and authors are made in the text as appropriate. A few of the recipes and a little of the text were used, in slightly altered form, in my column for *Gray's Sporting Journal*.

Introduction

A shrimp is a crustacean, cousin to the lobster and the crawfish (or crayfish). Several hundred species of shrimp live in warm water and cold, deep water and shallow, salt water and fresh. Jumbo shrimp—up to 9 inches long—even live in freshwater rivers, and tiny shrimp called doods—no longer than ⅛ inch—swarm in salt ponds found, believe it or not, in the Sahara Desert.

All true shrimp (including most of the large species that are sometimes called prawns) are decapods, having five sets of long legs used for walking. These are hung in two rows up front, under the head and thorax. Shrimp also have numerous shorter, paddlelike feet under the abdomen. Called piedpods, these are actually used for swimming in the water. Indeed, swimming is the shrimp's primary mode of transport, whereas the lobsters and crawfish, also decapods, are primarily bottom walkers and bottom feeders. Normally, shrimp dog-paddle forward, using their short legs. When frightened, however, they can scoot backward by flexing their abdomenal muscle (the part we eat), thereby working the tail fins. This action causes a rapid movement through the water—and can sometimes enable the shrimp to leap clear of the surface.

Shrimp have thin shells, making them easier to shuck and eat than lobster, crawfish, crabs, and most other shellfish. They also yield more meat per pound.

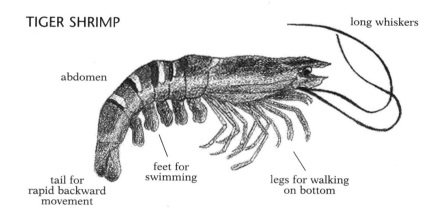

TIGER SHRIMP

long whiskers

abdomen

tail for rapid backward movement

feet for swimming

legs for walking on bottom

What's What

I would have liked to avoid this topic, because there's so much confusion about the various kinds of shrimp and prawns, making it easy to bog down here instead of getting to the good part—cooking and eating shrimp. But I'll have to make a few general statements before proceeding. In many cases we find the terms *river shrimp*, or *tidewater shrimp*, or *lake shrimp* being used instead of a proper name. Sometimes the names used in local areas don't mean a whole lot, partly because there are so many shrimp with similar names—*pink shrimp* or *tiger shrimp*, for instance. Further, color is not always a reliable guide to species. Some shrimp will take on the color of the bottom. In short, I don't see the advantage of trying to list all the scientific names here. I can, however, clear up one thing: A prawn is simply a large shrimp. These include the green tiger prawn, the yellow prawn, the banana prawn, the freshwater prawn, and others.

The one exception is the Dublin Bay prawn, which isn't really a shrimp. It's a small member of the lobster family, sometimes called scampi and sometimes *langoustine*. It lives in the waters of Northern Europe and perhaps elsewhere. Still, in some cookbooks—even some from Ireland—we see the terms *Dublin Bay prawn* and *jumbo shrimp* used interchangeably. They shouldn't be, for the texture of the meat and the thickness of the shell are different.

Be warned also that some "rock shrimp," which are not true shrimp, have a hard shell and a big, offensive sand vein. I think these are best when split lengthwise, deveined, and broiled, using a butter or olive oil baste and a little lemon juice.

As for the rest of the edible shrimp, I advise you to put more stock in freshness and size than in species or exact classifications. Some markets feature several different species of shrimp, but most of us won't have a wide selection at any one time. Because freshness is so important, having a good eye and a little experience with fresh shrimp is probably better, from a culinary viewpoint, than a degree in marine biology.

It's safe to say that a large part of the world's market shrimp are still caught in the Gulf of Mexico and the Atlantic waters of the Southeast. These include the brown shrimp, the white shrimp, the pink shrimp, and the red shrimp—and some of these were not even fished until after World War II, when the demand increased, partly because of the increased availability of frozen shrimp (sometimes breaded, ready for the skillet) in supermarkets hundreds of miles from the sea.

These days shrimp farming is helping meet the demand for more and more shrimp. It's not a new idea. In Asia shrimp have been raised in tidewater ponds for at least 500 years. Modern shrimp farming started in Japan during the 1930s, but it was profitable only because the Japanese are willing to pay exorbitant prices—up to $100 per pound, live—for the kurma shrimp, the shrimp of choice for eating live at raw bars.

Today various species of shrimp are being farmed quite successfully here and there around the world. In Asia the favorite crop is perhaps the giant tiger prawn, native to the Indian and southwestern Pacific Oceans. White shrimp are raised in several locations, along with western blue shrimp and others of color. Thailand has become a leader in shrimp farming, but the practice has also been successful in various other parts of the world. Some species of shrimp do better in the cooler climes, but in general the highest yields come from areas with warm weather and lots of rainfall. Temperate zones can average two crops a year, and farms along the equator can sometimes produce three. One unusual shrimp farm is in Arizona, where water from an old seabed is pumped into man-made growing ponds—with the runoff used to irrigate olive trees.

One old approach to shrimp farming, still in use, is to obtain egg-bearing females from fishermen. These are usually hatched out in nursery ponds or perhaps tanks; the young shrimp are then raised in holding ponds. Modern approaches include careful control of water quality, improved feeding techniques, and so on. It's quite scientific.

The shrimp growers, of course, claim that their product is superior to wild shrimp. I'm not prepared to go that far, but I will say that farmed shrimp are perfectly acceptable, especially if they're properly frozen for market immediately after the harvest, or at least sold and consumed very fresh.

Anyone interested in shrimp farming can find tons of practical and scientific information on the subject. Check out Shrimp News by e-mail at brosenberr@aol.com on your home computer or at the library. But don't get all starry eyed about the potential yield. Startup is expensive—and be warned that an entire crop can be wiped out by a large hurricane or a bacterial disease.

How Shrimp Are Caught

Until quite recently in man's culinary history, shrimp were taken mostly from shallow waters around the coastline. They can sometimes be caught in baited traps of one sort or another, just as lobsters and crabs are caught in baited pots, but historically most of the shrimp catch was made with cast nets or seines dragged through the water. At one time outriggers were used to extend nets out into the water from the shore; these were actually pulled along by horses or mules walking the beach. I've even heard of such a rig being used with a pickup truck fitted with large beach tires.

Of course, most of the catch these days comes from shrimp boats with booms on either side. These hold trawls—large baglike nets that are dragged through the water and sometimes over the bottom. The trawls scoop up the shrimp as the boat moves along. After the nets are hauled in at the end of a run, the shrimp are taken out and sorted. The rest of the catch is usually thrown back into the water.

Because shrimp are so perishable, commercial trawling in the Gulf of Mexico and South Atlantic waters developed only after the advent of mechanical refrigeration, deep freezing, and modern transportation. The first modern seagoing shrimp trawlers appeared about 1917.

Recreational shrimping isn't as popular as it once was, owing partly to the pollution of our bays and tidewater areas. But it's not completely a thing of the past. Small seines can be used, but round cast nets are perhaps your best bet. These are available in coastal areas, but be warned that practice is required to use them properly. It's best to learn from an old salt, or perhaps invest in a how-to video.

For the latest local information, check with "beer, bait, and baloney" shops along the coast and tidewaters. Some of these will give you more information than you need. Also check with the local fish and game authorities for rules and regulations, and possibly for pinpointing restricted areas.

Another possibility is shining—spotting the shrimp in shallow water at night, much like hunting frogs or crawfish in freshwater ponds. The hunter wades or boats along with a light strapped around his head, holding a long-handled pole with a special wire dipper or trap on the end. The light beam shines the eyes of the shrimp just under the surface of the water, several yards ahead. With luck and skill and a stealthy approach, the hunter can dip up the wary shrimp.

In any case, catching enough shrimp for a mess usually requires lots of hard work. Of course, a thorough knowledge of local conditions will increase your chances of success—even to jubilee status. Knowing where to go and when are just as important as how-to skills. As a general rule, it's best to bring along a few cans of sardines for eating purposes in case you don't catch enough shrimp for a midnight boil. If you do succeed in catching shrimp, however, try to keep them alive until the moment of cooking. If this isn't practical, at least put the shrimp on ice as soon as possible.

Market Forms

Shrimp are sold in various forms, from raw to cooked to fully shucked. My take is printed below, with the best choices listed first. I might add that my selection is made on purely culinary grounds, without regard to expense or convenience. Understandably, the working cook may choose prebreaded frozen shrimp for deep frying instead of shucking out fresh shrimp. This form of convenience cooking has become something of a trend in America. Look, for example, at what has happened to fish cookery. Most people—especially working women—prefer to buy fillets or breaded fish sticks instead of whole fish, simply because it's easier and less messy. If they lose the makings of a fish-head stew or a fish stock, so be it. It's the same with shrimp. It's understandable—but it's truly unfortunate from a culinary viewpoint. In any case, here's a breakdown listed in my personal order of preference.

LIVE SHRIMP

The best possible shrimp are dropped live into the pot. Unfortunately, live shrimp are simply unavailable except in some coastal areas, where they're used mostly as bait by fishermen. One exception is Japan, were shrimp are actually eaten alive or at least raw at the moment of beheading. Unlike lobsters, crawfish, oysters, some clams (those that close up tightly), and mussels, shrimp are difficult to keep alive even in suitable water. This makes live shrimp very expensive.

HEADS-ON RAW SHRIMP

These are the best choice for most home cooks simply because the head contains stuff—usually called "fat"—that adds to the flavor, juiciness, and color of shrimp dishes. As food scholar Copeland Marks has written, "Shrimp-head oil is considered a luxurious delicacy in Burma." In America, alas, it's usually a culinary treasure lost in the marketing process. Some coastal areas sell shrimp with the heads on, including them in the weight but offering to remove them for you (maybe they want the heads for themselves, or for reselling to pet food processors). Don't do it.

Some markets will sometimes have shrimp with heads on and sometimes with heads off. I really don't like this practice. In my experience, shrimp get soft after they have been out of the water for a couple of days, and the heads tend to come off during handling. Thus, I tend to suspect that heads-off shrimp in coastal areas are less than fresh. But this is a general statement, and there are no doubt many exceptions. It is certain, however, that refrigerated heads-on shrimp deteriorate quicker than beheaded shrimp.

In any case, my vote and my stand is for very fresh heads-on shrimp. You can easily behead them yourself before or after cooking; besides, the heads make very good stock. My dog Nosher also votes for leaving the heads on. She likes to eat them—especially from fried shrimp—and thinks them better and more nutritious than hush puppies.

BEHEADED RAW SHRIMP

These are sold with the tails and shells intact but the heads removed. When very fresh, they're great for boiling and peeling at the table, as well as for other recipes in which the shrimp are cooked in the shell.

It's also possible to purchase deveined raw shrimp in the shell. These are very easy to shuck at the table, but remember that opening up the top of the shrimp to remove the sand vein also permits more spice and seasoning to get into the meat. This feature may be highly desirable in dishes where shrimp are marinated for a short period of time. You may need to reduce the seasonings in other recipes, however—especially Cajun soaks.

SHUCKED SHRIMP

These are beheaded and peeled shrimp. They're often deveined. Although they don't have as much flavor after cooking as shrimp in the shell, they're very convenient for some recipes, especially frying. The tails are often left on for use as handles.

Deveined Shrimp

These are shrimp whose sand vein has been removed. They're usually fully peeled, but it's also possible to devein shrimp in the shell, either at home or at the market. The primary reason to devein shrimp is to remove the sand vein that runs through the body. Some people find this vein off-putting. This is usually a visual matter; folks who find the vein unappetizing in boiled shrimp shucked at the table might very well gobble them up in small fried shrimp without a thought. As often as not, the decision on whether to devein is based on the size and visibility of the vein. In any case, be assured that the vein and its contents are not going to hurt you, if the shrimp are fresh. If the veins or their contents were toxic, I would have been dead long ago. I have read in a very popular cookbook *(The Joy of Cooking)* that the vein can impart a bitter taste to the shrimp, but I've never noticed this. The same book, by the way, discusses frogs (or frogs') legs in the shellfish section.

Packaged Frozen Shrimp

Heretofore, most of the shrimp sold in supermarkets were shucked and frozen in small packages of a pound or less. While these can be good in some recipes, modern technology and mechanization offer greatly improved products, as discussed below.

Block-Frozen Shrimp

These are beheaded shrimp that are frozen in blocks either at the processing plant or at sea on large boats. If properly done, block freezing produces an excellent product. The keys are the freshness of the shrimp at the time of freezing, quick-freezing techniques, and keeping the shrimp inside the block unexposed to the air. Usually packaged in 5-pound or 2-kilo blocks, these are now available to consumers in larger markets and in some of the wholesale clubs.

If the truth be known, many of the so-called fresh shrimp in our markets are actually thawed block-frozen shrimp. I have no problem with this—I find it a better alternative to refrigerated shrimp that can't be moved within two days or so. Still, I feel that consumers ought to know what they're buying. Personally, I would much prefer to buy these in the frozen state.

In any case, a block or two of frozen shrimp makes a great way to hold a shrimp jubilee of some sort far from the sea. The only problem is in thawing the shrimp. Most seafood cookbooks recommend thawing any frozen fish or shellfish in the refrigerator—which will take two days with 5-pound blocks, and will create a drainage problem. I almost always thaw any frozen seafood under cold running water. Thawing them in open air or under warm water is not recommended because of possible bacterial contamination.

Sometimes you'll want only 2 pounds of shrimp from a 5-pound block. You can rinse the block under running water until enough shrimp can be pulled out, then refreeze what's left of the partly thawed block. But I have a better method: Cut off what you need with a saw. Better yet, consider the versatility of the next method of freezing shrimp.

INDIVIDUALLY QUICK-FROZEN SHRIMP

This is the latest and best way to freeze and market shrimp. Each shrimp is frozen individually and covered with a thin coat of ice. Then they're packaged and sold in bags or boxes. Since they're individually frozen, you can simply take out what you need and put the bag back into the freezer. These are also easy to thaw, as compared to block-frozen shrimp.

At present, individually frozen shrimp are available in the shell but are usually beheaded. I can only hope that heads-on shrimp will also become available in this form. If they can be frozen at sea, it seems to me that taking them out of the net and putting them into the quick freezer, without any beheading or other treatment except possibly for sizing, would be the way to go. We'll see.

Some supermarkets as well as wholesale clubs carry these shrimp. I expect the trend to continue. It strikes me as the best way to go, considering the perishability of fresh shrimp.

FROZEN BREADED SHRIMP

Available in the frozen-food section of every local supermarket, these are prebreaded and frozen shrimp ready for frying. They may also be available in some of the wholesale clubs in larger packages. Breaded shrimp are very convenient and can be quite tasty. Often they're available with the tails on, useful as handles for dipping into a little ketchup. Usually they are butterflied and deveined. Some of these can dropped into the frying pan without thawing. It's best to read the instructions on the package before proceeding.

PRECOOKED SHRIMP

I see precooked shrimp in the market. These are usually boiled or steamed and come fully shucked, ready to eat. Some are even arranged on a cocktail tray, white meats circled around a bowl of red cocktail sauce, maybe garnished with a few sprigs of green stuff. While precooked shrimp do indeed make for a convenient way to serve shrimp cocktails or shrimp salads for a crowd, I feel better—for safety's sake—about eating freshly cooked shrimp.

Precooked Frozen Shrimp

I prefer these to precooked unfrozen shrimp. They're sometimes arranged on serving trays. Simply thaw them out and serve.

Precooked Canned Shrimp

These are usually small, precooked shrimp. I like them in salads and sometimes in pasta dishes when only a few small shrimp are needed. They're tolerable when served with a red cocktail sauce.

Measures and Servings

Most modern cookbooks and magazine articles give "serving" recommendations. These are often a little vague, leaving the informed reader puzzled about whether the authors are talking about shrimp with the heads intact, beheaded shrimp, or fully peeled shrimp. It makes a big difference. In this book I try to list both beheaded shrimp and whole shrimp in the recipes. The former are the most readily available, but I'm convinced that the latter—heads-on shrimp—are the best way to go. Some recipes may work with either beheaded or fully dressed shrimp. The conversion formula below should help you determine amounts. It's not exact, but it's easy to remember and is close enough for all practical purposes.

2 pounds heads-on shrimp =
1½ pounds beheaded shrimp with tails intact =
1 pound fully peeled shrimp

Shrimp servings? I allow at least ¾ pound of beheaded shrimp per adult—and I'll want a few more. This greatly exceeds the serving portion recommended by most cookbooks and magazine articles. In fact, the word *serving* is often confusing simply because some people will want seconds. Thus "one serving" won't necessarily "serve one" person. In this book I use the term *feeds 2* instead of the ambiguous *serves 2* or *2 servings*. In most restaurants, true shrimp eaters—of which I am one—will have to order at least twice in order to fill up. There are no doubt exceptions in the restaurant trade, but I have found them to be few and far between. Besides, shrimp are easy to cook at home, on the patio, or on the tailgate along the coast, so why go hungry with restaurant servings? If price is a primary consideration when you're thinking about what quantity of shrimp you need, remember that most recipes in this book don't require lots of expensive ingredients. Also remember that smaller fresh shrimp are much cheaper than large ones, and can be quite tasty.

Sizing by Count

Most shrimp are graded by size somewhere along the line. There's no exact classification, but in general the larger the shrimp, the higher the price. This encourages the fishmonger to grade up whenever possible. I've seen jumbo shrimp that were merely large, by my count. Because of the confusion, some recipes call for shrimp by the count, as in "2 pounds of 16-to-20 shrimp" or some such notation. The same recipes may not be clear on exactly what they're talking about in the measure: that is, whether the shrimp should be heads on, tails on, completely shucked, or what, which would make a big difference in the count.

   Here's my take. The "doods" listed (somewhat whimsically) at the end of the scale are simply very tiny shrimp. My guess is that we will see more and more of these tiny shrimp being used in dried or paste form, or used to brew something similar to the fermented Asian fish sauces, all of which are quite tasty and highly nutritious. In any case, there's a thin line—one shrimp—between the various classifications of cookbook shrimp, and I suspect even more variation in the marketplace. I know one small fish market that seems to grade by whatever sizes they have in house on any one day. In other words, a jumbo is simply the largest they have on hand. Or so it seems. At any rate, the figures below are for heads-on raw shrimp.

super jumbo = fewer than 12 per pound
jumbo or extra large = 15 and fewer per pound
large = 16 to 20 per pound
medium = 21 to 25 per pound
small = 26 to 30 per pound
tiny = 31 to 40 per pound
doods = 41 to 100 or more per pound

Most small shrimp have very good flavor, but they don't shuck out much meat. It's just as easy to shuck a large one, making the larger sizes more appropriate for most recipes. In any case, the size you select for your table should depend on price and method of cooking and eating. When you're grilling, for example, small shrimp tend to fall between the slats, making jumbo the better choice. When you're cooking a casserole, by contrast, it's convenient to have bite-sized shrimp, whereas a jumbo would have to be cut before eating. The relation of size to recipe is discussed as appropriate in separate chapters on grilling, boiling, and so on.

Preparing, Serving, and Eating Shrimp

Don't worry. Properly cooked shrimp are easy to peel or shuck either at the table or in the kitchen. The exception is when shrimp are boiled or steamed too long, which causes the flesh to stick to the shell. There are gadgets to help peel shrimp, but these are really a waste of time and money. The fingers are faster, the licking better. In general, shrimp are much easier to peel or shuck than crawfish, lobsters, or crabs.

To shuck a shrimp, hold the meat part in your left hand (left-handers, of course, should reverse these directions). With your right hand, twist off the head, removing with it all the long legs still attached. Using your right-hand fingers, start peeling the shrimp from the bottom. The shell comes right off, taking the small abdominal legs or feet with it. The tail can be broken off before or after cooking, or it can be left on as a handle.

Shrimp are also the easiest things in the world to cook and serve. All you need (in addition to the shrimp) is a pot of boiling water, a little salt, brown bags for serving, and a few minutes' preparation time. A dip made with melted butter and lemon goes good with hot shrimp; a red cocktail sauce, with cold shrimp. Also, a loaf of chewy bread is a welcome addition to a shrimp boil, and a big tossed salad rounds out a meal.

For informal eating it's usually best to serve the shrimp in the shells, letting the diners shuck their own at the table. Most often, a pile of shrimp is put into the middle of the board, either on brown bags or on platters of some sort. The diners have individual plates, with small bowls for dipping sauces and other containers for holding the heads and peelings. Bread and salad or other go-withs can be served separately or perhaps on the plate with the shrimp.

People unaccustomed to this simple method of eating may be a little apprehensive at first about confronting whole shrimp at the table, and some will worry about the sand vein. After eating a few properly cooked shrimp, however, the novice quickly learns to shuck the shrimp in two seconds. After trying to remove the vein with knife or special tool, he will realize that the shrimp are getting cold and the pile in the middle of the table is going down fast while he fiddles with the sand vein. Before long he will forget the sand vein and start shucking and eating in unison with the rest of the company. A rhythm develops. Small talk at the table ceases as the diners hunker down to some serious eating.

Of course, this type of finger-licking eating is not appropriate for all occasions or all diners. Consider your guests. Some old hands at shucking beheaded shrimp at the table might be put off by heads-on shrimp, eyes bugging out. Sometimes a shrimp gumbo or a scampi will be more appropriate than boiled shrimp, partly because the shrimp will be fully peeled and even deveined. Fried shrimp, perhaps butterflied, are always good and might well be America's favorite restaurant seafood.

If deveining is necessary for the comfort of your guests, do it before or after the cooking, away from the table. Using a small paring knife, simply cut lengthwise into the shrimp from the top. The vein will be visible (if it isn't visible, why bother?) even before you make the cut. Lift the vein out with the tip of the knife. Many people who devein shrimp prefer to do so before cooking them, and the shrimp are usually held under running water during part of the process.

Clearly, having to remove the vein slows things down. Do it if necessary for the short-term comfort of your guests. For the long term, however, consider revising either the guest list or the menu. Hopefully, the chapters that follow will have something for everybody.

1

Shrimp on the Grill

I love to grill shrimp in the kitchen on an electric grill, but I really prefer cooking outside with chunk charcoal or wood. A simple open grill, such as a cast-iron hibachi, is all you need. Or merely rig a rack over some coals pulled away from a campfire. Some beaches provide picnic tables and open camp grills, and these can be used to grill fresh shrimp purchased nearby.

Be warned that small shrimp tend to fall through the slats of a grill. For this reason, large or jumbo shrimp are easier to grill, using tongs to turn them a time or two. Special small-mesh nonstick grates can also be used to contain smaller shrimp. Or you can use grilling baskets, which make smaller shrimp easier to turn. And don't forget kabobs, covered in chapter 9. In any case, turning small shrimp one at a time doesn't work too well, partly because the first of the batch will be done before you finish turning the rest.

For best results, cook the shrimp close to the heat source for 2 or 3 minutes on each side. This quick, hot cooking limits the application of smoke; on the other hand, the delicate flavor of fresh shrimp is easily overpowered by too much smoke. I usually prefer to grill shrimp in the shell, head and all, but this method doesn't work well with marinades. Beheaded shrimp and fully peeled shrimp will absorb more of the flavor of the marinade, if that's what you want. Deveined but unpeeled shrimp also pick up a lot of marinade.

The chef host of a TV show I once saw not only peeled and deveined the shrimp destined for his grill but also removed the tails. Why? He said they could be dangerous. His thinking was that someone might mistakenly eat the tails. Well, he should know that some people eat the tails on purpose, believing that they're just as good as fish fins. I would also like to point out that shrimp are often eaten shells and all in parts of Asia.

Here are some recipes to try. It's an honest selection, reflecting my belief that shrimp taste better than marinade and that usually 4 ingredients work better than 30.

SOY SHRIMP

Here's a favorite from the great American culinary sport James Beard. It calls for splitting the shrimp shell down the back with scissors and removing the vein. The shell and tail are left on. I also leave the heads intact, but suit yourself. By splitting the shell, of course, you allow the marinade to penetrate the meat.

1½ pounds beheaded raw shrimp, jumbo (2 pounds heads-on shrimp)	1 cup soy sauce 1 cup sake or dry vermouth

Split and devein the shrimp as described on page 28. Put the shrimp into nonmetallic container. Mix the soy sauce and sake, then pour the mix over the shrimp. Toss about to coat all sides.

Marinate in the refrigerator for 2 hours, tossing a time or two. Rig for grilling over high heat. Grill the shrimp for 3 or 4 minutes, turning once. Serve hot in the shell, along with several dipping sauces. Feeds 2 to 4.

HONEY SHRIMP

Owing to the marinade, this dish works better with shrimp that have been deveined but not shucked, as in the Beard recipe above.

1½ pounds beheaded raw
    shrimp, extra large or jumbo
    (2 pounds heads-on shrimp)
½ cup honey
⅓ cup freshly squeezed
    lemon juice

¼ cup melted butter
4 cloves garlic, minced
1 teaspoon cayenne pepper
    (or to taste)
salt to taste

Using all the ingredients except the shrimp and melted butter, mix a marinade and pour it over the shrimp in a nonmetallic container. Toss about to coat all sides. Marinate in the refrigerator for 1 hour or a little longer, turning several times. Rig for grilling over coals or gas. The heat should be quite high. Grease the grilling rack. Dip each shrimp into the melted butter and place it on the grill, working quickly. Grill for 2 minutes, turn, and baste with melted butter. Grill for another 2 minutes or so, turn, baste, and check for doneness. The shrimp should be nicely pink with a brown spot or two. Do not overcook. Serve hot. Feeds 2 as a main course, or several as an appetizer.

SHRIMP MOZAMBIQUE

Several countries in both East and West Africa use a hot chili and oil sauce for marinating and basting seafoods. It's especially good as a baste for grilled large shrimp. This particular recipe is from Mozambique, where grilling over an open fire or charcoal is popular. I like to use small red Tabasco or cayenne peppers freshly picked from my own garden, but use any fresh red chili peppers of your choice. Be careful, though: Some of these peppers are pure fire. If you need to dilute the peppers, add more oil or butter and lemon juice to the measures below. Remember that the peppers should be seeded and the hot pith removed from the inside. And don't forget to wear rubber gloves or wash your hands when you're done; the pepper oil will burn you. Use large shrimp that have been beheaded, peeled, and deveined. Leave the tails on, but do not butterfly. You'll need a grill large enough to hold all the shrimp without overlapping them. The grill need not have a cover, making it easy to rig any sort of rack over hot coals.

2 pounds beheaded raw jumbo shrimp, shucked, with tails left on*
4 fresh hot red chili peppers
1 cup olive oil
juice of 2 medium to large lemons

4 cloves garlic, crushed and minced
1 tablespoon chopped fresh parsley or cilantro
salt and black pepper to taste

The night before cooking, seed and chop the chili peppers, being careful to remove the inner pith (which contains lots of heat). Mix the chopped peppers with the lemon juice, garlic, and parsley in a small bowl. Refrigerate overnight.

Rig for grilling over charcoal or wood coals. Heat the hot pepper sauce with the olive oil in a small pot, keeping it warm for use as a basting sauce. When the coals are ready, adjust the rack to about 4 inches above the heat. Arrange the shrimp close together but do not overlap. Grill for 2 minutes—but do not cover. Baste lightly, turn the shrimp quickly, and grill for 2 minutes. Baste and turn again, cooking for 1 minute, or until done. Do not overcook. Serve hot. Feeds 2 to 4.

*If you start with heads-on shrimp, you'll need 4 pounds.

AUSTRALIAN TIGER PRAWNS

The Australians have their own terms for cookery, and American books on the subject don't always make things clear. A crawfish is a *yabbie*. A grill is a *barbie*. To broil (under the heat) is to *grill,* and a broiler is a *griller*. A broiling pan is a *barbecue plate*. One pretty cookbook has several recipes for prawns—but shrimp isn't even listed in the index, an omission that might well cost us some good cooking. (See the Hemingway recipe on page 41 for more complaints about indexing.) Yet shrimp paste and dried shrimp are discussed in a glossary. In any case, the Aussies are fond of grilled seafood, whatever it's called.

2 pounds fully peeled and deveined raw shrimp, jumbo*
1 cup butter
¼ cup freshly squeezed lime juice
¼ cup dry white wine
1½ tablespoons honey
1 tablespoon grated fresh gingerroot
1 tablespoon grated onion
finely ground sea salt to taste
Hungarian paprika
lime halves (for garnish)

Rig for grilling over charcoal or wood coals, or perhaps on an electric indoor grill. Melt the butter and stir in all the ingredients except the shrimp, lime halves, and paprika. Place all the shrimp on the grill and baste with butter sauce. Grill for 2 minutes. Turn, baste, and grill for 2 minutes. Turn, baste again, and cook for another minute, or until the shrimp are nicely pink. Sprinkle lightly with paprika. Serve with lime halves. Feeds 4.

*It's best to clean your own, starting with 3 pounds of beheaded shrimp or 4 pounds of heads-on shrimp.

GOOD OL' BOY GRILLED SHRIMP

This tasty treat works best with fully peeled shrimp and thin-sliced bacon. Thickly sliced bacon takes too long to cook; if you do use it, cook it in a skillet until it's about half done. Because the bacon will drip, these taste treats are best cooked on a large grill and moved about as needed, making this a hands-on kind of cooking. It's true that cooking these in a grill with a closed hood will help prevent flare-ups, but the results won't be quite the same.

extra-large shrimp, shucked	**lemon-pepper seasoning salt**
thin-sliced bacon	**beer**

Rig for grilling over charcoal or gas heat. Sprinkle each shrimp lightly with lemon-pepper seasoning salt, wrap in half a strip of thin bacon, and secure with round toothpicks. Dip each shrimp quickly into the beer. Grill for 8 to 10 minutes, turning from time to time and moving about with tongs. Servings? Allow ½ pound of shucked shrimp and a beer or two for each person.

Note: Try cooking these with a long stick over a beach fire. Omit the seasoning salt, but dip the bacon-wrapped shrimp in seawater before grilling.

SAIGON SHRIMP

This easy recipe calls for whole shrimp that have been deveined, partly to permit some of the marinade to get inside. Jumbo shrimp work best for deveining. If you must, use beheaded shrimp, in which case the deveining step can be omitted because the shrimp will be open on their big end to the marinade.

1½ pounds beheaded raw shrimp, jumbo (2 pounds heads-on shrimp)	1 tablespoon sea salt
	1 tablespoon freshly ground white pepper
¼ cup lime juice	dipping sauce

Devein the shrimp and place them into a nonmetallic container. Mix the lime juice, sea salt, and white pepper. Pour over the shrimp, cover, and let the shrimp marinate for 20 minutes or so. As they marinate, rig for grilling over charcoal. Arrange the shrimp on the grate and grill for 2 minutes on each side. Serve hot with a suitable dipping sauce, such as Nuoc Cham on page 177. Feeds 2 or more.

A. D.'S POMEGRANATE SHRIMP

I'm fond of cooking with the juice from pomegranate seeds, and with a sweet-and-sour syrup made from the juice. Some of the pomegranate molasses imported from the Middle East can be used, but in my experience these concoctions, or at least some of them, have a cloudy color and an off taste. I think they're made from the whole pomegranate, squeezing the pulp as well as the seeds. In any case, fresh pomegranates can be obtained in American supermarkets. I am fortunate enough to have my own trees, and I was raised on a farm with five trees, all with pome-granates of a slightly different tartness.

1½ pounds beheaded raw
shrimp, extra large (2 pounds
heads-on shrimp)

1 ripe pomegranate
½ cup melted butter
sea salt

Rig for grilling over charcoal. While you're waiting for the coals to heat up, cut into the pomegranate (or break it in two if it has split open on the tree) and remove all the seeds from the pulp, being careful not to get the juice onto your clothing—it will stain. Divide the seeds into two piles, discarding the peeling and inner pith. Using a mortar or sieve, mash the juice from one of the piles; strain out the juice, discarding the pulp. Mix the juice into the melted butter, and heat to use as a basting sauce. Reserve the rest of the seeds. Brush the shrimp lightly with the sauce and place on the grill. Cook for 2 minutes, turn, and baste. Cook for another 2 minutes, turn, baste again, and sprinkle lightly with fine sea salt. Cook for another minute or so, or until the shrimp are nicely pink. Serve hot on a bed of rice, along with grilled eggplant and other go-withs. Garnish with the rest of the pomegranate seeds. I allow at least ¾ pound of beheaded shrimp per person, but you can get by with a smaller amount if you have plenty of eggplant.

MESQUITE SHRIMP

Some chefs make much ado about what kind of wood chips to use for flavoring meat on the grill and even set forth all kinds of subtle descriptions of flavor. I won't say these people are dishonest; they just have a vivid imagination and (like wine critics) a large vocabulary of adjectives. I think any good hardwood will do for cooking shrimp or even fish. Most people simply buy a bag of chips at the supermarket and use them as needed, with or without soaking them in water. I prefer freshly cut wood chips or chunks. But it just doesn't make that much difference, at least not to me.

If you have guests coming for a shrimp feed, however, you can't go wrong by dropping the name *mesquite* or *mesquite-smoked shrimp*. Purists, of course, will point out that mesquite is far too robust for shrimp, and that what you really need for shrimp and escargots is the sweet mellowness of maple. Suit yourself, but remember that shrimp cook very quickly, and they don't pick up much smoke in 3 or 4 minutes. Cooking them longer, over indirect heat, tends to make them dry and tough, and too much smoke overpowers the natural flavor. In any case, it's best to peel the shrimp for this one.

1½ pounds beheaded raw shrimp, jumbo (2 pounds heads-on shrimp; 1 pound fully dressed shrimp)

hardwood chips
¼ cup melted butter
juice of 1 lemon
sea salt

Soak some hardwood chips in water. Rig for grilling over gas or charcoal, or perhaps on an outdoor electric grill. Behead and shuck the shrimp, saving the heads and peelings for stock (page 181) if wanted. Devein if you must. Mix the lemon juice and melted butter. Place the shrimp onto the hot grate. Baste lightly. Cook for 2 or 3 minutes. Turn, baste lightly, sprinkle lightly with sea salt, and grill for 2 minutes, or until the shrimp are nicely pink. Serve hot, along with a dipping sauce. Servings? I allow ¾ pound of beheaded shrimp per person.

A. D.'S GRILLING MACHINE SHRIMP

I'm fond of using the George Foreman grilling machine (which cooks top and bottom at the same time, like a waffle iron) for cooking a few large shrimp for myself or possibly for a meal for two. It's very, very easy, and tasty. This method of cooking isn't really grilling, but it doesn't fit into the other chapters either.

Any good basting recipe can be used, but I like to keep it simple, using a few fresh herbs from my garden.

beheaded raw shrimp or   **fresh dill weed**
   heads-on shrimp,   **lemon juice**
   large or jumbo

Preheat the grilling machine. Place the shrimp close together and baste lightly with lemon juice. Lay two or three sprigs of dill over the shrimp. Close the hood and cook for 2 or 3 minutes, depending on the size of your shrimp. Do not overcook. Serve hot with vegetables, salad, and so on. Have on the table two hand mills loaded with peppercorns and coarse sea salt for those who want to grind a twist or two of either. I allow at least ¾ pound of beheaded shrimp per person.

Note that the smaller-sized grilling machine doesn't hold enough shrimp to feed even one big eater. The largest size works best for shrimp, burgers, steaks, and most other food if two or more people are to be served. Of course, these things cook very quickly, making it practical to cook more than one batch.

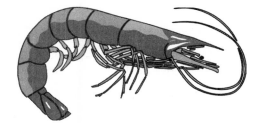

2

Shrimp in the Boil

Listen. If you'll cock your ear toward southern Louisiana and listen hard, you can hear the Cajuns starting to yell before I say a word here. Still, I'll hold the spices and fire ants until we get to individual recipes. Just the shrimp, salt, and water required for a boil will give us plenty to talk about for openers. Even so, it's hard to find common ground, simply because there's more than one way to boil a shrimp.

If there is one single point on which most shrimp cooks and shrimp eaters agree, it's this: Do not boil the shrimp too long. If you do, they'll be dry and tough—and, just as important, hard to peel. By comparison, a properly cooked shrimp, still hot from the boil, will burst with sweet juices when you bite into it, and it'll be so easy to shuck that you and your guests waste no time going from one bite to another.

The best shrimp for the boil are very fresh heads on, large or perhaps jumbo. The smaller shrimp are tasty, it's true, but they require more work for what you get. (I fondly remember eating some small shrimp in Cuba years ago, together with a group of my fellow sailors. We ate half a day, until the café ran out of shrimp, and never got our fill of either the shrimp or the Cuban beer. Apparently the energy expended in shucking the shrimp was more than we consumed, so that the longer we sat, the hungrier we became.)

My next choice for the boil is very fresh beheaded shrimp, unpeeled. Properly frozen fresh shrimp are also good for boiling. Peeled shrimp don't work as well, simply because they don't retain the natural juices.

In any case, fresh shrimp and water are all you need for a memorable boil. A little salt helps. How much salt to use varies from one boil to another, one method to another, one cook to another. As a rule, the longer the shrimp are in the water, the more salt they will absorb. (This is also true of spices, a good point to remember unless you want pickled shrimp.) If the shrimp are in the boil for only 2 or 3 minutes, however, the salt won't penetrate the shell very much—in which case the water should be quite salty. The measure of salt should also depend on how much water is in the pot. If the shrimp are beheaded or deveined, the salt is in direct contact with the meat, so that you don't have to use much.

A good deal also depends on how the shrimp will be served and eaten. If they'll be shelled at the table, each man for himself, they shouldn't be rinsed after the boil. Instead, pile them on a brown bag steaming hot. A little of the salt will remain on the shell and come off on the fingers during the shucking. That's what you call finger-licking good. If the shrimp are to be shucked away from the table, chilled, and used in a salad, the salt from the boil will be pretty much lost.

So, again, your approach should be influenced by how the shrimp will be served. I want mine with the heads on, but I realize that the heads are off-putting to some people. I also realize that heads-on shrimp are not readily available in some markets.

In this case, beheaded shrimp are much better than no shrimp at all.

As a general rule, the shrimp should be boiled for only 2 or 3 minutes, or until they turn pink. Remember that water boils at 212 degrees at sea level. Turning up the heat will make the water boil away faster—but it won't get hotter under normal conditions. The water will, however, get hotter under pressure; going the other way, it won't reach 212 degrees at high altitude, where the pressure is less. Still, I like to boil at a very high heat, causing the shrimp to bounce around in the pot.

Serving boiled shrimp as a meal is an easy, informal affair—or should be. Simply pile them steaming hot (unrinsed) onto large platters or even brown bags. Provide a plate for each person, along with small cups for dipping sauces. Also provide a large bowl or container or some sort for the heads and shells. Salad, bread, and other go-withs are best served in a separate bowl, leaving the whole plate for a pile of shrimp.

Cold shrimp are a little different and are usually—but not always—consumed in smaller quantities as an appetizer or as noshing fare along with beer. These are sometimes peeled before serving, sometimes not.

THE WORLD'S BEST COLD SHRIMP

While doing my homework for this book, I dipped into the recipe index of *The Hemingway Cookbook*, by Craig Boreth. There was no shrimp entry. While browsing about in the text, however, I happened upon a recipe in the "Key West and Cuba" chapter called Prawns in Sea Water. Well, hell. The recipe itself plainly lists "2 pounds prawns (with heads still attached) or jumbo *shrimp*" and the instructions say "add the prawns or *shrimp*." And around the recipe itself is much talk about shrimp and the Royal Order of Shrimp Eaters—founded, I understand, by Hemingway, with membership gained only by eating a whole shrimp, head and all. Clearly, Ernest knew the score, but for one reason or another "shrimp" and the "Royal Order of Shrimp Eaters" got overlooked by the compiler of the index. The omission damn near cost me dearly. But all's well that end's well, I guess.

If seawater isn't readily available for this world-class recipe, use ordinary water and sea salt.

1½ pounds beheaded raw
  shrimp, jumbo or large
  (2 pounds heads-on shrimp;
  fully peeled won't do)
1 quart seawater (or more;
  see next recipe)

ice water
¼ cup fresh lime juice
2 limes, quartered
  (for garnish)
6 whole black peppercorns

Bring the seawater to a boil in a large pot, adding the peppercorns and lime juice. Add the shrimp, bring to a new boil, and cook for about 5 minutes, or until the shrimp turn bright pink. Do not overcook. Remove the shrimp and plunge them into a bowl of ice water. Drain and serve, garnished with lime quarters.

The book says that this recipe makes 4 servings. Like most other books published during the past 15 years or so, however, it fails to indicate how many "servings" are required to satisfy a good man. I suspect that Ernest Hemingway could have easily eaten the whole batch. I know I can. After all, 2 pounds of wet heads-on shrimp will yield only 1 pound of meat.

WORLD'S BEST HOT SHRIMP

The Hemingway recipe above can be improved—if I may dare presume—by using more water for boiling the shrimp. Of course, hot shrimp are also best with a butter and lemon sauce used as a dip.

3 pounds beheaded raw   Butter and Lemon Sauce,
  shrimp, large or jumbo   warm (page 174)
  (4 pounds heads-on shrimp) hot crusty bread
2 gallons or more seawater

Bring the seawater to a boil in a large pot. Put in the shrimp, bring to a new boil, and cook for 3 minutes, or until the shrimp turn nicely pink. The exact time will depend on the size of the shrimp and sometimes on your altitude. Drain on a brown bag. Serve the shrimp hot along with plenty of warm lemon butter sauce and hot crusty bread and perhaps a large tossed salad. Feeds 4, if you've got plenty of bread.

BO JOHN'S BEST

Bo John Lester is something of a legend around my hometown of Wewahitchka, Florida, where he's known as one of the best shellcracker fishermen in recorded history. On the subject of fishing you can't believe a word he says, especially when he gives directions to a newly found bream bed. His talk about cooking fish and seafood is generally straight, however, and he even agrees with me that boiling a fresh shrimp is the best thing you can do to it—and the worst. It's a matter of degree. As previously stated, boiling a shrimp too much makes it difficult to shuck and tough to chew. But how to arrive at perfection is open to debate. Here's Bo John's method, using beheaded shrimp, if you can believe that.

very fresh shrimp,   water
  heads on or off   salt

Bring a big pot of water to a rolling boil over high heat. Add some salt. Pinch the heads off the shrimp, if necessary. Put the shrimp into the water. Bring to a rolling boil. Turn off the heat and let the shrimp sit in the hot water until they're cool enough to shuck. Enjoy.

THE MEMPHIS BOIL

A culinary sport by the name of W. L. Nichol IV let go of this recipe in *A Man's Taste,* published by the Junior League of Memphis. Bo John Lester says that the recipe's method and its thyme are hard to believe, but I tested it out to my satisfaction.

1½ pounds beheaded fresh shrimp, large (2 pounds heads-on shrimp)	½ head garlic, peeled
	5 cloves
2 quarts heavily salted cold water	a pinch of thyme
	a pinch of basil
1 rib celery with leaves, chopped	Tabasco sauce to taste

Put the salted water—cold—into a pot. Add the rest of the ingredients. Turn on the heat, bring to a boil, and cut off. Let the shrimp coast in the water for a few minutes, making sure they are nicely pink. Serve hot or chilled. Feeds 2 or more.

IRISH SHRIMP

Billed as Dublin Bay Prawns in the recipe title, the ingredients list for this recipe (reworked here from *Irish Cooking,* by Ethel Minogue) calls for jumbo shrimp—live. I've cooked the dish successfully with shrimp that were a little less than live—but they should be very fresh.

2 pounds live shrimp, jumbo
 (1½ pounds beheaded
 shrimp)
1 cup butter
6 cloves garlic, minced

lemon wedges
freshly snipped parsley
salt and freshly ground
 black pepper
1 gallon seawater or salt water

Bring the water to a rolling boil in a pot. Drop in the shrimp. Bring to a new boil. Cook for 1 minute. Drain the shrimp. Heat the butter and garlic in a saucepan, adding a little salt and freshly ground black pepper. Add the shrimp and cook for 3 minutes, stirring as you go. Serve hot, garnished with lemon wedges and parsley. These go nicely with brown bread and stout. Feeds 2. Be warned that this is a finger-licking recipe, with or without amorous intent.

THE SCANDINAVIAN BOIL

The Scandinavians love boiled crawfish and lobster flavored with a little dill. The same recipes work for shrimp, but with reduced boiling time. I usually use fresh dill seed heads, snipped from plants just outside my back door. These heads are used whole, unchopped, making the measures easy but imprecise because the size of the heads varies quite a bit. If chopped, a head would probably yield about 1 tablespoon of fresh dill weed.

1½ pounds beheaded fresh
 shrimp, large or extra large
 (2 pounds heads-on shrimp;
 1 pound fully peeled shrimp)

1 gallon water
1 cup sea salt
fresh dill heads or chopped
 dill weed to taste

Bring the water to a boil. Add the salt and 1 dill weed head. Boil for 2 minutes. Add the shrimp. Bring to a new boil, add another dill weed head, and cook for 3 minutes. Remove the pot from the heat, cover, and let cool in the dill water for 10 hours.* Serve cold, garnished with fresh dill. Serve these as appetizers—or on the smorgasbord table.

*Be warned that beheaded shrimp and peeled shrimp will take up lots of dill and salt over such a long soaking period.

OUTER BANKS SHRIMP BOIL

This simple recipe came from the Outer Banks area of North Carolina, where the old salts know their shrimp. Be sure to try it.

1½ pounds beheaded raw shrimp, medium to large (2 pounds heads-on shrimp)	1 dry pod hot red pepper
	4 cups water (or more)
	vinegar
3 tablespoons salt	black pepper

Crush the red pepper into flakes with a mortar and pestle. Bring the water to a boil in a pot, adding the crushed pepper and salt for a few minutes. Add the shrimp. Bring quickly to a new boil. Cook for 3 or 4 minutes, until the shrimp turn pink. Drain. Mix a dipping sauce by simply adding black pepper to taste to a little vinegar. Peel the shrimp at the table and dip into the vinegar mixture. Feeds 2 to 4.

MAYAN SHRIMP

The Mayans of the Yucatán and surrounding areas are fond of using annatto seeds (or *achiote*) as a seasoning and a red food coloring, just as mild paprika is used in some quarters. The seeds (as well as a paste) are available in Latin American spice markets. In the street and dock markets of modern Veracruz, boiled shrimp are sold in brown paper cones, much like the fish-and-chips of England. Also, shrimp boiled in salt water with annatto seeds are popular ingredients in a large seafood platter, along with crab legs, oysters, and seviche made with local saltwater fish. The recipe below covers only the shrimp.

3 pounds beheaded raw
  shrimp, large (4 pounds
  heads-on shrimp)
1 gallon seawater (or plain
  water with 1 cup sea salt)

1 tablespoon annatto seeds
4 limes, halved
Tabasco sauce

Put the water into a pot, add the annatto seeds, and bring to a boil. Add the shrimp, bring to a new boil, and boil for 3 minutes. Then let the shrimp sit in the hot water for 3 minutes. Drain. Refrigerate. Serve whole, along with lime slices and a bottle of Tabasco sauce. As each shrimp is peeled, squeeze onto it a drop of lime juice and one of Tabasco. Feeds 4 or more.

NEW ORLEANS SHRIMP

The swankier New Orleans chefs like to boil heads-on shrimp in something more than spiced salt water, calling it court bouillon.

1½ pounds beheaded raw
  shrimp, large or extra large
  (2 pounds heads-on shrimp)
1 gallon good water
1 cup salt
½ cup freshly squeezed
  lemon juice
1 tablespoon chopped
  celery leaves

1 tablespoon chopped
  fresh thyme
2 teaspoons freshly
  crushed allspice
2 teaspoons freshly ground
  black pepper
1 teaspoon Tabasco sauce
½ teaspoon dry mustard

Put all the ingredients except the shrimp into a pot over high heat. Boil for 10 minutes. Add the shrimp. Bring to a new boil for 3 or 4 minutes, depending on the size of the shrimp. Drain and serve the shrimp hot, warm, or chilled. Serve with several dipping sauces, along with lemon wedges. Feeds 2 or more.

THE CAJUN SOAK

The Cajuns have made a profession of mixing and selling spices for crab, shrimp, crawfish, and other seafoods. The mixes, either liquid or bagged spices, are widely available these days in supermarkets and fish markets. In some supermarkets the mixes are found in either the seafood section or the spice section, or perhaps both. Your results with these mixes depend not only on how much of the mixture you use but also on how long the shrimp stay in the liquid. My copy of *The Official Louisiana Seafood & Wild Game Cookbook*, published by the Department of Wildlife and Fisheries, recommends 15 minutes of soaking for a mild flavor; 30 to 45 minutes for a heavier flavor. The recipe below calls for 1 bottle of liquid crab boil, which I presume is 4 ounces of the stuff. You can also use shrimp boil or a combined crab and shrimp mix. (It's also best to read the directions on the bottle, since concentrations differ and may change in the future.) I use a Zatarans liquid seasoning, which is widely distributed. Note that the recipe calls for shrimp, crab, and crawfish, all of which require different boiling times. Note also that the crawfish and crabs work best if they're dropped into the boil while still alive. The recipe can also be prepared with all shrimp, which should be very fresh. In any case, this is a good recipe for outdoor cooking, using a gas-heated turkey fryer or some such rig. Make two batches in two cooking rigs if needed, or increase as needed. One good cook can handle three rigs if he has a big wooden paddle and a large handheld strainer.

Generally, allow 1 pound of undressed shellfish per person. You'll need more, along with plenty of beer, for Cajuns and good ol' boys of all sorts.

5 pounds heads-on raw shrimp, medium to large

5 pounds heads-on crawfish, live

5 pounds blue crabs, live

3 large onions, chopped

3 lemons, thinly sliced

2 ribs celery with green tops, chopped

6 bay leaves

1 bottle liquid crab or shrimp boil (4-ounce size)

ice cream salt to taste (2 cups or more)

2 cups ice water

Fill a large pot three-quarters full with water and bring to a boil. Add all the ingredients except the shellfish and ice water. Cover the pot and boil for 10 minutes, until the flavors mix. Add the shrimp. Boil for 4 minutes. Remove the shrimp to drain. Boil the crawfish for 5 minutes. Drain. Boil the crabs for 12 minutes. Put all the shellfish back into the pot and stir about with a paddle. Add the 2 cups of ice water, which will cause the shellfish to settle down in the pot (instead of floating on top) and better absorb the seasoning (if that's what you want). Depending on how much spice flavor you want, soak for up to 45 minutes. If in doubt, shuck and taste a shrimp from time to time. Drain and serve immediately at outdoor temperature or chill for later use.

Note: Dry Cajun spices can also be used instead of liquid, following the directions on the package. Brand names include Tony Chachere, Paul Prudhomme's, and Konriko. See also the next two recipes.

CAJUN JUBILEE

Professional Cajuns have large vats of one sort or another for boiling crawfish, and these work nicely for shrimp and crabs. As often as not, a wooden boat paddle, unvarnished, is used for stirring. Fortunately, the large pots marketed these days for frying whole turkeys also work for shrimp, and one cook can work two or three of these at a time to feed a crowd of people, as indicated in the previous recipe. It's best to dump the boiled shrimp onto an outdoor table, perhaps covered with brown bags, and let the eaters dig into the steaming pile while the cook prepares another batch.

Another method is to dump the boiled shrimp into a Styrofoam cooler, which will keep them hot for several hours. Be warned that the heat can warp plastic coolers. I like this method with plain boiled shrimp, using only salt water. The shrimp can be put into the cooler a layer at a time, each sprinkled with Cajun Dust (page 180), lemon-pepper, or seasonings of your choice. If you have more than one container, vary the seasonings, giving your guests a choice.

For safety, make sure that the cookers are stable and keep them well away from the crowd, especially if you're entertaining Cajuns, beer-drinking good ol' boys, or children. A large pot of boiling water is dangerous.

A complete rig for boiling lots of crawfish, shrimp, and crabs includes a 15-gallon pot with a lid, a sturdy gas burner, two propane or butane tanks, a wooden paddle for stirring, and a basket or strainer that fits into the pot, so that the contents can be removed easily. It's very important that the burner be adequate for the job. Smaller camp stoves don't put out enough heat to boil the water properly. The recipe below has been adapted from *Cajun Men Cook*, published by the Beaver Club of Lafayette, Louisiana.

20 pounds heads-on shrimp,
 large (15 pounds beheaded
 raw shrimp can be substituted,
 but cut back on the spices or
 reduce the soaking period)
7 gallons water

½ pound ice cream salt
 or sea salt
8 ounces liquid shrimp or
 crawfish boil (or to taste)
1 small box cayenne pepper
 (1½-ounce size)

Rig for boiling outdoors with a 15-gallon pot. Light the gas, pour the water into the pot, add the seasonings, cover, and bring to a rolling boil. Put the shrimp into the strainer insert and carefully lower into the pot. Cover the pot and bring to a new boil. (This will take several minutes; keeping the cover on the pot will speed up the process. Just don't forget to check frequently for the boil.) Boil the shrimp for 3 minutes. Turn off the heat and let the shrimp soak for 3 minutes. Remove the strainer and either dump the shrimp out onto a suitable table or put them into a large Styrofoam cooler to keep them hot. Servings? Allow at least 1 pound of heads-on shrimp per person.

If you need a second batch of shrimp, re-season the water with ¼ pound of salt, ½ cup of crab or shrimp boil, and about ½ ounce of cayenne. Bring to a boil and insert 20 pounds of shrimp in the strainer. Repeat until the crowd is full, or, more likely, until all the shrimp are boiled. Also, it's easy for a cook to attend more than one burner-pot-strainer unit, if needed. Using several cookers is not unusual at a real Cajun boil for a crowd, where live crawfish are used instead of or in addition to shrimp, along with some live blue crabs. (You'll need 5 pounds of crawfish per person.) Such feasts also feature boiled corn on the cob, new potatoes, onions, carrots, and perhaps some spicy sausage. Eat as much as you can, then settle it all down with half an ice-cold watermelon. Find a good shade tree and take a nap.

THE CAYENNE BOIL

Here's an interesting variation on the boiled-shrimp theme, using lots of cayenne pepper. If you like hot stuff, try the whole measure; if not, cut back on it or consider passing on this one. The technique, however, can be used with other ingredients.

3 pounds beheaded fresh shrimp, large (4 pounds heads-on shrimp)
1 gallon hot water
1 cup cold water

1 cup salt
¼ cup cayenne pepper (or to taste)
1 lemon, sliced
1 onion, sliced

Put the gallon of hot water into a large pot. Add the onion, lemon, and cayenne. Bring to a boil. Add the shrimp. Bring to a new boil for 3 minutes. Cut off the heat. Add the cold water to stop the boil, then stir in the salt. Let sit for 5 minutes. Drain the shrimp (but do not rinse) and serve warm or cold. Feeds 4 or more.

THE ONE-POT FEED

I am fond of cooking shrimp and corn on the cob or new potatoes with a few links of highly spiced smoked sausage, all boiled in the same pot. The sausage provides the seasoning.

beheaded raw shrimp or heads-on shrimp, large
smoked link sausage, cut into 3-inch segments

fresh corn on the cob or new potatoes
small onions, peeled
water
salt (but not too much)

When you're rigging for the boil, remember to limit the salt to the amount you'd normally use to boil corn or potatoes. Bring the salted water to a boil. Add the corn or new potatoes, sausage, and onions. Cover the pot and boil until the corn or potatoes are tender, letting the sausage and onions take care of themselves. Add the shrimp and bring to a new boil. Boil for 3 minutes. Remove all ingredients, piling them all together on a suitable table. Have ready paper plates, bread, and small cups of sauce or dips. I allow about a pound of shrimp per person.

Notes: You can use other vegetables in the boil, even broccoli, if you or your guests feel guilty about pigging out on shrimp, sausage, and corn. Note also that you can mix crabs, crawfish, and shrimp in the pot, using a countdown schedule. Large crabs, for example, are usually boiled for 12 minutes. To mix them with shrimp, put them into the pot, boil for 9 minutes (12 minus 3), add the shrimp, bring to a new boil, and boil for another 3 minutes. Be warned that some market crabs and crab claws (especially from stone crabs) are precooked. Put these in with the shrimp, allowing the 3 minutes to heat them up properly. Do not overcook these. Many market crawfish are also precooked. If they're cooked again, they aren't good and will not compare to crawfish put into the pot while still alive.

FROZEN SHRIMP BOIL

Most of the recipes in this chapter can be prepared with properly frozen shrimp, duly thawed. Somewhat shockingly, frozen shrimp can also be cooked successfully by putting them directly into a pot of boiling water. This works nicely for individually frozen shrimp or for shrimp in a block of ice, provided that the package isn't too big. Simply put the shrimp into the boiling water, along with salt and other seasonings, if desired. Bring the pot to a new boil, then cook for a minute or two, until the shrimp turn nicely pink. Turn off the heat and let them sit for a few minutes, then remove the shrimp and drain. Serve hot or cold, or use in recipes calling for boiled shrimp.

I don't recommend this method, but I'll have to admit that I have used it successfully on a number of occasions when I didn't have time to thaw the shrimp. My guests didn't seem know the difference—but I did. In any case, much depends on how fresh the shrimp were at the time of freezing, and on how they were frozen. When I find really fresh shrimp, I usually buy more than I need for the occasion and freeze the surplus in 1-pound units. I almost always freeze these in a block of ice, using a plastic container of suitable size. In recent years I've started freezing very fresh shrimp (purchased in 50-pound lots from a local fellow who owns and more or less professionally operates a small shrimp boat) in vacuum-pack bags. These thaw out quicker than those frozen in a block of ice. With a new batch in the freezer, unexpected company doesn't have to rely on potluck.

3

Shrimp in the Steamer

There's a difference between boiled shrimp and steamed shrimp. Boiling is by far the more common method of cooking shrimp, but *steamed shrimp* apparently looks better on the recipe, menu, or other bill of fare. A perfect example of what I'm talking about comes from a book on food festivals. Covering the Annual Shrimp Festival at Gulf Shores, Alabama, the text had a recipe titled Steamed Shrimp. Here are the directions for the cooking: "Fill a large pot with water and bring to a boil; stir in the remaining ingredients [salt, black pepper, cayenne, bay leaf, and lemon juice] and add the shrimp. Cover and boil over medium high heat for about 5 minutes, or until the shrimp change color (they should turn bright pink). Remove from the heat and serve immediately." Well, these are clearly boiled shrimp, not steamed. I have a few other questions about the recipe, too, partly because it calls for a pinch of salt and a dash of pepper. I doubt that the residents of Gulf Shore would be so stingy on the salt, and maybe not on the pepper. Apparently the shrimp the authors ate at Gulf Shores had been beheaded, but I know as absolute fact that at least some of the residents in that area will want the heads left on. True, heads-on shrimp might be off-putting at the festival—but the authors of the book go a step farther. They tell us to rinse the shrimp but leave the shells intact—adding that the feet can be removed before cooking! Can you believe that? I suppose you could cut the feet off with kitchen scissors, but why? They come right off with the shell.

Shrimp are steamed by putting them in or over a small amount of water. It's important that the pot be quite hot and the water at a rolling boil before the shrimp are added. Also, a tightly fitting lid is highly desirable. A sealed pressure cooker will work—but remember that the heat increases with the pressure. A wok fitted with a bamboo steamer can also be used, but this may take a little longer than a metal pot with a tight lid. I normally use a 5-quart pot without a rack in the bottom, letting the shrimp on the bottom rest in, but not covered by, the shallow water. You can stir the shrimp a time or two with an upward motion, to get more of them to touch the bottom and thereby pick up a little salt and other seasonings—but do not stir or remove the lid more than a time or two. If you do, you'll lose your head of steam.

A rack can be used to keep the shrimp from touching the water, if that's what you want. Using a basket to hold the shrimp also works, but it should be heated in the pot before you add the shrimp. After steaming, use the basket to remove the shrimp from the pot.

Remember that steam can burn you badly. Open the lid away from your face, always.

SHRIMP BALTIMORE

I understand that the heads are removed in most variations of this recipe. Suit yourself. Only a small amount of liquid is used, so no special rack or steaming rig is necessary. It's best—almost essential—to have a tightly fitting lid, however. The pot should be about 5-quart capacity.

2 pounds beheaded raw shrimp, large	**½ teaspoon dry mustard**
½ cup white vinegar	**½ teaspoon ground allspice**
½ cup cold water	**¼ teaspoon ground bay leaf**
2 teaspoons salt	**¼ teaspoon ground celery seeds**
½ teaspoon black pepper	**¼ teaspoon mace**
½ teaspoon paprika	**⅛ teaspoon dried ginger**
	⅛ teaspoon cardamom

Heat the water and vinegar in a pot of suitable size. Add all the spices and seasonings. Bring to a boil. Add the shrimp, stir about with a large wooden spoon or spatula, and cover the pot tightly. Reduce the heat to medium. Stirring a time or two with an upward motion, steam for about 6 minutes, or until the shrimp are nicely pink. Remove the pot from the heat and pour off the liquid. Let the shrimp cool in the pot to room temperature. Serve as a meal or appetizer. For a meal, allow ¾ pound of heads-off shrimp per person.

BEER-STEAMED SHRIMP

I see this recipe name listed on the menu at seafood eating houses from time to time, especially along coastal areas. Any beer will do, but this statement will be hotly contested in some quarters. You will need a 5-quart pot with a tightly fitting lid. A rack can be used to hold the shrimp off the bottom, but this isn't necessary.

1½ pounds beheaded fresh shrimp, large or jumbo (2 pounds heads-on shrimp)	**finely ground sea salt**
	Butter and Lemon Sauce, warm (page 174)
1 bottle beer	

Heat the pot and add about half the beer. Bring to a hard boil. Add the shrimp, cover tightly, and steam for 3 or 4 minutes, depending on the size of the shrimp. Uncover, add the rest of the beer, and stir with an upward motion. Cover and steam for 2 minutes. Uncover. The shrimp should be nicely pink. Steam another minute or two if necessary. Sprinkle with finely ground sea salt, tossing about. Serve steaming hot, along with the melted dipping sauce. Allow ¾ pound of beheaded shrimp per person.

BEACHCOMBER'S SHRIMP

In some areas the knowledgeable fisherman can get a few pounds of shrimp from beaches or tidal creeks with a cast net, sometimes throwing while wading or perhaps from a bridge or pier. If not, really fresh shrimp—and sometimes live shrimp—can often be purchased from local fish markets. At my favorite shrimp and oyster town—Apalachicola, Florida—there are a dozen small retail as well as wholesale markets along Highway 98. Some of these establishments are rather large; others are shacks or roadside stands. In any case, this recipe was inspired by another local delicacy, small and little known, called coquinas. These are clams about 1½ inches long that travel in loose schools along the breaking surf. They can be spotted, with a sharp eye, in the receding surf as they wiggle into the sand. Once located, they can be scooped up by the hundreds. The local people make a broth with these—sometimes called Apalachicola Cocktail—and I go a step farther, as in this recipe.

Larger clams can also be used. With the tiny coquinas, however, only the juice is eaten. The meats are too small to fool with.

2 pounds heads-on raw   **fresh lemon juice**
   (or beheaded) shrimp,   **Tabasco sauce**
    medium to large   **water**
2 gallons coquinas   **salt**

Put the coquinas into a large stockpot. Add enough water to almost cover, along with a little salt. Bring to a boil. Add the shrimp, cover, and steam for 4 minutes or so, or until the shrimp are bright pink. Stir with an upward motion a time or two during the cooking. Using a large hand strainer, remove the shrimp but retain all the coquinas and broth. Serve the shrimp steaming hot. I allow a pound of shrimp per person.

Save all the heads and peelings from the shrimp. When you've finished eating shrimp, add the heads and peelings to the pot. Bring to a new boil, cover, and simmer for 15 minutes or so, letting the shrimp heads flavor the coquina broth. Let the broth cool, then strain it, mashing the shrimp heads in a sieve to get all the juice. Serve in individual bowls, adding a little lemon juice and Tabasco sauce to taste. If you prefer, refrigerate the sauce and eat it later.

Actually, I consider the recipe for Beachcomber's Shrimp to be only a suggestion. Use your imagination—and remember that extra-large shrimp will work in a New England–style clambake, in which the shrimp are actually steamed instead of baked. If you're got shrimp and wet seaweed, you've got the makings of a memorable steam.

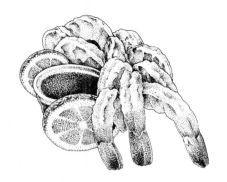

4

Shrimp in the Oven

Baking in the kitchen is ideal for cooking large chunks of meat, such as roasts and turkey, and for casseroles. Whole shrimp, being relatively small, are usually cooked by another method. But there are some exceptions and surprises.

When you're baking anything in an oven it's best, almost without exception, to place the meat in the center, where the heat is more even. The top of the oven gets hotter simply because heat rises, and the bottom puts the baking pan too close to the heating element, where radiant heat comes into play. In any case, make sure that your oven thermostat is reasonably accurate, or, if it isn't, learn to make adjustments. There are several inexpensive oven thermometers that you can use to check on the thermostat setting.

I don't recommend cooking shrimp in a microwave, partly because they cook so quickly in regular ovens and by other methods.

Enough said. A New Orleans shrimp recipe has haunted me for years, and I am eager to get to it.

NEW ORLEANS "BARBECUE"

I first ate this dish about 30 years ago, when I worked for two weeks in New Orleans. I was in not a swanky restaurant in the French Quarter, but a luncheon nook in a large drugstore. I was pleased with the dish—finger-licking good—but puzzled as to why it was called a "barbecue." I still puzzle over the matter. The dish was simply baked in the oven and served in its own spicy sauce. The shrimp were whole—heads on—and had to be peeled at the table, which added to the gustatory experience as you licked your fingers. Since then I have seen several recipes for "barbecued shrimp," and in all of them the method of cooking doesn't seem to indicate a real "barbecue." Indeed, it seems that any shrimp cooked whole and peeled at the table is "barbecued." While I heartily endorse the method, I do question the name of the dish. In any case, be sure to try this recipe, calling it what you must.

This dish can be made with beheaded but unpeeled shrimp, but the effect is simply not the same. The fat in the head contributes to the sauce, and New Orleans culinary sports will indeed suck the fat out of the heads, just as they do with crawfish.

2 pounds heads-on raw shrimp, medium to large (1½ pounds beheaded shrimp)
¼ cup butter
¼ cup olive oil
¼ cup Worcestershire sauce
juice of 2 lemons
6 cloves garlic, minced
2 tablespoons Creole or Cajun seasoning
1 tablespoon freshly ground black pepper
salt

Rinse the shrimp and set them aside to drain. Preheat the oven to 400 degrees. In a saucepan, heat the butter and add the rest of the ingredients except the shrimp. Cook and stir for a minute or so, then remove from the heat. Put the shrimp into a baking pan with sides about 1 inch deep, spreading evenly. Ideally, the shrimp should cover the bottom but not overlap. Pour the sauce over the shrimp, stirring them about for even coating. Put the pan in the center of the hot oven and bake for 3 minutes. Turn the shrimp quickly and bake for another 3 minutes, or until they're nicely pink. Serve in large soup bowls, pouring a little of the pan sauce over each serving, along with hot New Orleans or French bread for sopping any remaining sauce from the bowl. A huge tossed salad on the side makes this a complete meal. Feeds 2 or more.

Note: Some recipes call for adding Tennessee sour mash bourbon, but I really prefer to sip this while I cook.

SHRIMP AND FISH FILLETS

When making this dish, I like to start off with whole fish and whole shrimp. This permits me to make a nice stock. A suitable stock, however, can be made with either the fish or the shrimp trimmings, or both. It's best to use rather small fish, giving you enough fillets to layer in the baking pan or oven-proof dish. I use a Pyrex dish about 6 by 9 inches square, suitable for serving.

4 pounds small bass or
other suitable fish, whole
1½ pounds beheaded fresh
shrimp, small (2 pounds
heads-on shrimp)
1 medium onion, sliced
1 medium carrot, sliced
4 ounces fresh mushrooms,
sliced

2 cups milk
1½ cups cracker crumbs (divided)
¼ cup flour
¼ cup butter (divided)
½ cup grated cheddar cheese
3 freshly ground allspice berries
salt and white pepper to taste
water

Preheat the oven to 325 degrees. Fillet the fish. Behead and shuck the shrimp. Set the fillets and dressed shrimp aside, putting the trimmings into a pot with about 4 cups of water, along with the carrot and onion. Boil for half an hour or so, then strain the stock, discarding the solids. Poach the fillets in the stock for 5 minutes. Drain. Poach the shrimp for 3 minutes, or until they turn pink. Drain. Measure the broth and either boil it down or add a little water to make 2 cups. Set aside. Melt 3 tablespoons of the butter in the saucepan. Stir in the flour slowly. Add the milk, stock, salt, allspice, and white pepper. Stir in about half of the cracker crumbs. Add the shrimp and mushrooms. Lightly grease a baking pan or dish. Make a layer of fish fillets in the pan, using about half. Spoon on the shrimp sauce, spreading it evenly. Top with the rest of the fillets. Mix the rest of the cracker crumbs with the butter and spread on top. Sprinkle on the grated cheddar. Bake in the center of the oven for 25 minutes, or until the top is nicely brown. Serve hot. Feeds 4 to 6. For similar recipes using shrimp as a stuffing, see chapter 13.

STUFFED SHRIMP

This dish works best with crabmeat, as listed in the ingredients, but it can also be made with white-fleshed fish that have been poached and flaked. Sheepshead is especially recommended as a substitute for crabmeat, and there are several imitation crabmeats on the market. Jumbo shrimp work best for stuffing.

1½ pounds beheaded fresh
   shrimp, jumbo (2 pounds
   heads-on shrimp)
½ pound crabmeat
1 cup milk

½ green bell pepper, seeded
   and finely chopped
2 tablespoons flour
2 tablespoons mayonnaise
2 tablespoons sake or sherry

6 tablespoons butter (divided)	1 teaspoon Worcestershire sauce
1 medium to large onion, finely chopped	1 teaspoon dry mustard
½ red bell pepper, seeded and finely chopped	salt and black pepper
	paprika
	freshly grated Parmesan

Preheat the oven to 350 degrees and grease a large, shallow baking pan. Dress the shrimp, leaving the tails on, and split each one down the middle to butterfly, removing the vein as you go. (Save the shrimp heads and peelings for stock, if desired for another recipe.) In a saucepan, heat 4 tablespoons of the butter and sauté the onion and bell peppers for 4 or 5 minutes. Add the crabmeat, mayonnaise, mustard, Worcestershire, salt, and black pepper. Stir and set aside. In a small saucepan or skillet, melt the remaining 2 tablespoons of butter. Add the flour and milk, stirring as you go. Stir in the wine. Add this mixture to the crab mixture and blend well. Stuff each shrimp with the crab mixture and arrange in the greased baking pan. Dot with more butter and sprinkle lightly with Parmesan and paprika. Bake in the center of the oven for 25 to 30 minutes, or until the cheese is golden brown. Feeds 4 to 6 as the main part of a meal.

SHRIMP DE JONGHE

This classic American dish, rich with butter, can be cooked in a casserole dish suitable for serving, or in individual oven-proof serving dishes. I understand that the recipe originated in Chicago, which got its name from the wild onion and garlic that once grew so profusely in the area. Consequently, the last time I made this dish I substituted ½ cup of chopped wild garlic with tops for the garlic cloves and green onions. It was delicious.

1½ pounds beheaded fresh shrimp, medium (2 pounds heads-on shrimp)

1 cup dry bread crumbs (divided)

½ cup melted butter

frozen stick butter

½ cup dry vermouth

¼ cup chopped fresh parsley

¼ cup chopped green onions with tops

4 cloves garlic, minced

1 teaspoon chopped fresh thyme

1 teaspoon chopped fresh basil

1 teaspoon chopped fresh tarragon

salt and freshly ground black pepper

Preheat the oven to 425 degrees and grease a casserole dish suitable for serving. Behead and peel the shrimp, saving the heads, tails, and shells for stock if needed for another recipe. Reserve 2 tablespoons of bread crumbs, and mix the rest with the shrimp, vermouth, melted butter, parsley, green onions, garlic, thyme, basil, tarragon, salt, and black pepper. Spread the mixture into the dish and sprinkle with the reserved bread crumbs. Grate a little of the frozen butter on top, distributing it evenly. Bake in the center of the oven for about 10 minutes, until the shrimp are nicely pink and the topping is lightly browned. Serve hot. Feeds 4 to 6.

GREEK SHRIMP

Here's a Greek recipe calling for lots of feta cheese and a delicious tomato sauce. The dish can be baked in shells of the sea scallop (those of the bay scallop aren't quite large enough) or in individual ovenproof serving dishes or ramekins. The number of shells you'll need depends on their size, but 6 or 8 will be about right. I think it's best to prepare 2 for each diner.

3 pounds beheaded fresh
  shrimp, medium to large
  (4 pounds heads-on shrimp)
½ pound feta cheese
½ cup tomato sauce
¼ cup olive oil
¼ cup chopped fresh parsley
3 medium tomatoes, chopped

juice of 1 lemon
1 medium onion, minced
2 cloves garlic, minced
1 tablespoon chopped fresh dill
salt and freshly ground
  black pepper
parsley sprigs (for garnish)

1. Peel and devein the shrimp, saving the heads, tails, and peelings for stock, if desired (page 181). Sprinkle the peeled shrimp with lemon juice. Set aside.

2. Preheat the oven to 350 degrees and grease scallop shells or ramekins with a little of the olive oil.

3. In a skillet or saucepan, heat the olive oil and sauté the onion for about 5 minutes. Add the garlic, tomatoes, tomato sauce, chopped parsley, dill, salt, and pepper. Simmer for 25 minutes. Push through a sieve and reserve the liquid for use as a sauce.

4. Arrange the shells or dishes on a shallow baking pan, making sure they won't topple easily. (Some ice cream salt will help if you're using scallop shells.) Spoon a little of the sauce into each shell and fill with shrimp, dividing equally. Pour some sauce over the shrimp and top with crumbled feta. Bake for 15 minutes in the center of the oven. Finish off under the broiler for a few minutes. Serve hot, garnished with sprigs of parsley. Have ready a huge tossed salad topped with black olives.

SHRIMP AU GRATIN

I like to prepare this dish with whole shrimp and shrimp pieces, about half and half. This gives it a texture befitting an au gratin.

3 pounds beheaded shrimp,
   medium (4 pounds heads-on
   shrimp)
2 cups milk
1 cup grated sharp
   cheddar cheese
¼ cup butter

¼ cup flour
¼ cup sherry or dry vermouth
2 tablespoons sugar
1 tablespoon Hungarian
   paprika
salt and pepper to taste
slivered almonds

Dress and devein the shrimp, reserving the heads, tails, and peelings for stock (page 181) if desired. Mince about half the shrimp, leaving the rest whole. Preheat the oven to 325 degrees. Grease an ovenproof dish suitable for serving the au gratin. Melt the butter in a saucepan and, with a wooden spoon, stir in the flour. Slowly add the milk and sherry. Stir in the sugar, salt, and pepper. Bring to a boil, then quickly remove from the heat but keep warm. Place about half the whole shrimp and half the chopped shrimp into the dish. Top with about half of the cheddar. Pour in about half the butter sauce. Add the rest of the whole and chopped shrimp. Add the rest of the cheese and top with the rest of the butter sauce. Sprinkle with paprika and slivered almonds. Bake in the center of the oven for about 45 minutes. Feeds 4 to 6.

5

Shrimp Under the Broiler

The process of cooking shrimp under a source of heat, usually an electric coil, might at first seem the same as cooking them over the heat. But there are differences. Shrimp grilled over the heat, as over charcoal, can take on a smoke flavor from the wood or from juices or oil dripping onto the coals or heat source. Of course, this can be a plus for grilling, up to a point. Another plus is that grilling can be done over an open fire (with the hood of the grill open), letting the cook see what's going on and permitting him to turn the shrimp or kabobs easily. Hence, grilling is, or can be, more of a hands-on kind of cooking.

Still, broiling can produce some very tasty shrimp indeed, and the method can add something that's missing from grilling. I'm talking about pan broiling, in which the shrimp are in contact with the bottom of a broiling pan. This lets the shrimp baste in the pan juices during the cooking process, and results in some memorable eating, as I hope the recipes below show.

Broiling on a rack is also an option, in which case turning the shrimp can be a small problem. Using extra-large or jumbo shrimp make the process easier. Indeed, smaller shrimp might be in danger of falling through the rack's slats. A basket can be used to hold the shrimp, in which case the whole works is removed from the broiler oven, turned, and put back in. Even a long-handled grilling basket can work, because you can leave the oven door open during broiling. The shrimp can also be strung up on kabobs for easy turning; see chapter 9 for details.

Note that true broiling works best with the heating element on high and the oven door slightly open. If you cook in a closed oven, you are partly baking the shrimp—which may be perfectly satisfactory as long as you realize what you're about. Gas ranges can be used for broiling under the flame, but often you have to get on your knees to use these. In either case, it's best to broil with the shrimp close to the heat source—usually no more than 3 or 4 inches. Also, remember to preheat the broiler before use.

In any case, broiling is a very good way to cook a few shrimp. I use it often in a small auxiliary oven/broiler when I'm cooking for only one or two people.

PAN-BROILED SHRIMP

Here's a dish to cook for people who don't mind peeling their own shrimp, but object to the sand veins. It works best with jumbo shrimp, preferably with the head still on.

1½ pounds beheaded fresh shrimp, jumbo (2 pounds heads-on shrimp)	6 cloves garlic, minced
1 cup olive oil	1 tablespoon freshly ground black pepper
¼ cup freshly squeezed lemon juice	salt

Wash the shrimp, cut each one down the back with a small, sharp knife, and remove the sand vein. (Do not cut deeper than necessary—just a little over halfway. Make your cut in the middle; you can see the black vein once you start the cut. This process may be a little easier if you cut the shell down the back with small kitchen shears before making the slit with a knife.) Mix all the other ingredients and pour over the shrimp in a nonmetallic container. Marinate for about 2 hours in the refrigerator.

Preheat the broiler and adjust the rack so that the top of the shrimp will be about 4 inches from the heat. Place the shrimp into the broiling pan and pour the marinade over them. (They should fit snugly but should not overlap.) Broil for 3 minutes. Turn and broil for another 2 or 3 minutes, or until the shrimp are done. Do not overcook. (The exact time will depend on the size of the shrimp and the heat of your broiler.) Serve hot, along with rice pilaf, vegetables, salad, and crusty bread. Have plenty of napkins for those diners who don't want to lick their fingers at the table. Feeds 2 to 4, depending on go-withs and appetite.

SOY-BROILED SHRIMP

Soy sauce, one of the most useful ingredients the cook can keep on hand, has made steady gains in American cookery. Like mayonnaise and ketchup, it has truly become a part of our cuisine either on its own or as an ingredient in steak and stir-fry sauces. This recipe works nicely for people who object to peeling shrimp at the table and are sensitive to the sand vein.

3 pounds beheaded raw shrimp, large to jumbo (4 pounds heads-on shrimp; 2 pounds fully peeled shrimp)
1 cup soy sauce
olive oil
juice of 2 lemons
1 tablespoon vinegar
1 tablespoon finely grated onion
2 cloves garlic, finely grated
cayenne pepper to taste

Dress and devein the shrimp. (Save the heads, tails, and peelings for stock, if wanted; page 181.) Mix the soy sauce, vinegar, lemon juice, grated onion, and grated garlic. Preheat the broiler. Arrange the shrimp in a broiling pan. Add enough olive oil to reach a depth of ¼ inch. Pour the soy mixture over the shrimp, distributing it evenly. Sprinkle with cayenne. Broil about 4 inches from the heat for 5 or 6 minutes, more or less, depending on the size of the shrimp. Do not overcook. Remove the shrimp to a serving dish and pour the pan drippings over them. Serve hot. Feeds 4 or more.

SCAMPI BROIL

These shrimp can be prepared on a broiling rack or in a broiling pan. I prefer the latter, with the pan placed about 4 inches from the heat source. (For a skillet scampi, see page 88.)

1½ pounds beheaded raw shrimp,
   large or jumbo (2 pounds
   heads-on shrimp; 1 pound
   fully dressed shrimp)
1 cup butter
½ cup fresh chopped parsley

¼ cup olive oil
juice of 1 lemon
6 cloves garlic, minced
salt and freshly ground
   black pepper
Hungarian paprika

Dress and devein the shrimp, saving the heads, tails, and shells for stock if wanted for another recipe (page 181). Preheat the broiler. Place the shrimp in the bottom of a broiling pan. Mix the rest of the ingredients, except for the paprika, and pour over the shrimp. Broil for 4 minutes. Turn, sprinkle lightly with paprika, and broil for 3 minutes more. Serve hot, along with plenty of rice pilaf, vegetables or salad, and bread. Feeds 2 or more.

DILLED SHRIMP

Fresh dill, sparingly used, imparts a unique flavor to crawfish and shrimp, as the Scandinavians know. I like to combine butter and fresh dill in a sauce. Note that this recipe calls for extralarge shucked shrimp. The tails can be left on or removed. Deveined or not, as you please.

2 pounds shucked shrimp, jumbo*

½ cup butter

2 tablespoons freshly snipped dill weed

sea salt to taste

Melt the butter in a saucepan. Add the dill and sea salt. Simmer for a few minutes, then set aside and keep warm. Preheat the broiler, rigging the rack about 3 inches from the heat. Arrange the shrimp on the rack. Broil for 2 minutes, baste, and broil for another 2 minutes. Turn, baste, and broil for about 3 minutes. Baste and broil for 1 minute, or until the shrimp are done and have turned nicely pink. Serve immediately with a huge tossed salad containing some freshly sliced cucumber and generous slices of garlic bread. Have a pepper mill on the table. Feeds 3 or 4.

*If you want to shuck your own, start with 4 pounds of heads-on market shrimp or 3 pounds of beheaded shrimp.

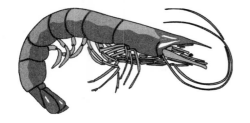

6

Shrimp in the Deep Fryer

For true deep frying, the oil should be quite hot and deep enough to float whatever is being cooked. Thus, deep frying for shrimp can be accomplished with 3 inches of oil, whereas a whole turkey would require much more. The more oil, the better, up to a point, so that adding a new batch of shrimp to the pot won't lower the temperature very much.

A stovetop Dutch oven or other suitable pot can be used to deep fry on a kitchen stove, but for feeding a crowd nothing beats the oblong fish fryers and tall turkey fryers heated by propane or natural gas, designed for outdoor cooking. Indoors or out, a grease or candy thermometer fitted onto the deep fryer makes the process more foolproof. Be warned, however, that a large pot of boiling grease is dangerous. (So is a skillet filled with hot oil.) Keep a box of baking soda handy for emergency use; pouring a little onto burning oil will produce carbon dioxide, which will quickly extinguish the flame. Do not use water. Electric deep fryers with a thermostat are safer, but some of these don't get hot enough to suit me.

Most modern vegetable oils are suitable for deep frying. I use peanut oil more than any other because it has a rather high smoke point, it's tasteless (contrary to what is said in some other cookbooks), and it doesn't absorb odors from the food. For economy, I use it several times. After each fry, I usually strain it through paper coffee filters. Olive oil is an excellent choice for deep frying; it has more flavor than peanut oil or other vegetable oils. Sesame cooking oil, now commonly seen on supermarket shelves, is suitable—but it should not be confused with the Asian sesame oil, which is made with roasted seeds and has a dark color and strong flavor.

Draining fried shrimp properly is almost as important as the frying. There are various baskets that fit into the deep fryer for cooking and then quickly removing the shrimp or other food. I seldom use these because I often don't want to take up the whole batch at a time, and I don't want the food too crowded while draining. I think brown paper bags work best for draining, with the shrimp separated from each other. I like to pick up large shrimp with tongs, letting each one drain a second or two over the pot. Then I place it on the brown bag for further draining. After a few minutes, I pile the drained shrimp together to make room for more and to help hold in the heat while the rest of the batch cooks. Tongs are too slow to use with small shrimp, however. For these I use a slotted spoon or a handheld strainer.

As a rule, large shrimp destined for the deep fryer should be beheaded, shucked, and butterflied with the tail attached. The tail acts as a handle. Smaller shrimp can also be fried with the tails on, but they make an easier bite if the tails are removed—unless you like the tail's crunch. I know people who do.

Some cookbooks recommend that shrimp be boiled and shucked before they're fried. Don't do it. This is probably a carryover from crawfish cookery, in which the boiling makes it easier to remove the shells. Shrimp are easier to shuck, and precooking them before frying is a culinary sin. Indeed, a cardinal rule is: Don't overcook your shrimp. They're done when they float, although a few more seconds in the hot oil may be required to brown them properly, especially if the shrimp were cold or frozen when you put them into the deep fryer or skillet. If in doubt, cook a little longer. How long? Until the shrimp are golden brown. If the oil is hot enough, 2 minutes of total cooking time is all it takes for medium to large shrimp. If the oil isn't hot enough, longer cooking will be required, and the shrimp may become tough and chewy before the outside browns.

BREADED SHRIMP

Here's a good recipe to use for feeding a crowd. The measures below will do for 3 or 4 people, but the recipe can doubled or enlarged as needed. Note that the shrimp can be breaded and refrigerated long before it's time to cook, which simplifies the recipe if you're cooking outdoors or feeding a crowd. If you're picnicking, consider serving this one in a newspaper cone, like the British fish-and-chips, along with french fries.

1½ to 2 pounds beheaded fresh shrimp, large (2 to 3 pounds heads-on shrimp)
¾ cup fine dry bread crumbs
¼ cup flour

2 tablespoons vodka
1 chicken egg
salt and cayenne pepper to taste (used twice)
peanut oil for deep frying

1. Dress the shrimp, leaving the tails intact and saving the heads and peelings for stock (page 181), if needed for another recipe. Set the shrimp aside.

2. Get out a bowl and two small bags. In the first bag, mix the flour, salt, and cayenne. In the bowl, beat the egg with the

vodka. In the second bag, mix the bread crumbs with a little salt and cayenne. Shake the shrimp, a few at a time, in the flour mixture. Dip them one by one into the egg mixture, holding by the tail, and drain off any excess. Shake them in the bag of bread crumbs a few at a time. Set aside or refrigerate until you're ready to cook.

3. Rig for deep frying, heating the peanut oil to 375 degrees. Fry a few shrimp at a time until golden brown. Drain on a brown bag and serve hot, perhaps with a dipping sauce of your choice. A really good tomato ketchup goes nicely with breaded shrimp.

A. D.'S CORNMEAL SHRIMP

Be warned that this recipe works only with fine cornmeal, preferably white and stone ground. The gritty yellow stuff put out by the large milling companies won't stick to the shrimp without the aid of whisked egg or some such goo.

medium shrimp	**fine white cornmeal**
peanut oil for deep frying	**salt and cayenne pepper to taste**

Shuck and devein the shrimp, leaving the tails on for handles. Rig for deep frying at 350 degrees. Dust the shrimp with salt and cayenne, then shake in a bag with the cornmeal. Shake off any excess cornmeal and fry the shrimp, a few at a time, for 2 or 3 minutes, or until they float and turn nicely brown. Drain on a brown bag and serve hot.

I like to allow ½ pound of shucked shrimp per person, but most people can get by with ⅓ or even ¼ pound if you serve plenty of french fries and bread.

MEME'S FRIED SHRIMP

Some of the best shrimp I've ever eaten in a restaurant were served up at Meme's on the Bon Secour River in Mobile Bay, Alabama, where the shrimp boats dock and where summer jubilee takes place. I purchased Meme's cookbook and have enjoyed its quaintness over the years almost as much as the shrimp. Their fried-shrimp recipe (as published in the book) calls for pancake mix. I have changed this to pancake batter made from a commercial pancake mix, according to the directions on the box. You'll want about 2 cups of batter. Always use fresh shrimp, the book says; cooked shrimp won't do.

THE SHRIMP SOAK
1 chicken egg

1 cup milk

juice of 1 lemon

½ teaspoon hot red pepper sauce (such as Tabasco)

1 teaspoon salt

THE SHRIMP
3 pounds beheaded raw shrimp, medium to large (4 pounds heads-on shrimp; 2 pounds fully dressed shrimp)

pancake batter

cracker meal

grease or vegetable oil for deep frying

Mix the soaking sauce ingredients. Dress and devein the shrimp, leaving the tail fins intact for use as handles. Put the shrimp into a nonmetallic container. Pour in the soaking sauce, tossing with your hands to coat all sides. Refrigerate for at least 1 hour, preferably longer. Rig for deep frying at 350 degrees and drain the shrimp. When the oil is hot, dip each shrimp into the pancake batter, roll it into cracker meal, and, using the tail as a handle, drop it carefully into the hot grease. Do not overcrowd. Fry until golden brown and drain on a brown bag. Serve hot. Feeds 4 to 6. Increase or decrease the measures as needed.

ORANGE BATTER SHRIMP

Here's an excellent recipe with a mild flavor. I like it cooked with medium shrimp, which, when dressed, require only a couple of minutes in hot oil to turn golden brown.

2¼ pounds beheaded raw shrimp, medium (3 pounds heads-on shrimp)
1 cup fresh orange juice

1 cup all-purpose flour
1 chicken egg, whisked
1 teaspoon salt
peanut oil for deep frying

Shuck the shrimp, leaving the tail fins intact and saving the trimmings for soups and stocks. Devein the shrimp if you are to serve squeamish diners. Rig for deep frying, heating 3 inches or more of peanut oil to 350 degrees. While the oil heats, mix the egg, flour, orange juice, and salt. Dip each shrimp into the batter and drop them into the hot oil one at a time—but move quickly so that the first one doesn't cook too much before the last is added. Do not overcrowd. Drain on a brown bag and serve hot, garnished with lemon wedges. Feeds 3 to 6.

COCONUT SHRIMP

Some people, including Forrest Gump, use beer instead of orange juice in this recipe, and pancake mix and flour instead of bread crumbs. Suit yourself.

3 pounds beheaded raw shrimp, medium (4 pounds heads-on shrimp)
2 cups finely shredded dry coconut
2 cups fine dry bread crumbs

½ cup orange juice
½ cup thick coconut milk
2 large chicken eggs
peanut oil for deep frying
salt and pepper to taste

Shuck and devein the shrimp, leaving the tails intact and saving the heads and peelings for Shrimp Stock (page 181) if needed for another recipe. Rig for deep frying at 375 degrees. In a bowl, combine the chicken eggs, orange juice, coconut milk, shredded coconut, bread crumbs, salt, and pepper. Holding them by the tail, dip each shrimp into the batter and drop into the bubbling oil. Do not overcrowd the fryer; cook several batches if necessary. Fry until the shrimp are golden and crisp, about 3 minutes. Drain on a brown bag and serve hot. If you want a sauce, try a Rémoulade Sauce (page 179) or Tartar Sauce (page 176). I allow ¾ pound of beheaded shrimp per person, but most cookbooks recommend smaller servings.

JAPANESE SHRIMP TEMPURA

I have mixed feelings about this classic dish, said to have come to Japan in the 16th century from Portuguese traders, who also brought a similar dish to Brazil. The success of the recipe depends, in large part, on a light, fluffy batter. Recipes for tempura batter abound, with some calling for a special self-rising cake flour, but my favorite has been adapted from *The Pleasures of Seafood*, by Rima and Richard Collin. Note that assorted fresh vegetables, dipped into the batter and deep fried, are a traditional part of the tempura. Another key to tempura's success depends on having a cold batter and a hot oil. Get the oil hot before frying the shrimp and fritters, and fry only a few at a time.

THE SHRIMP

1½ pounds beheaded raw shrimp, medium (2 pounds heads-on shrimp)	1 cup flour peanut oil

The Batter

2 large chicken eggs, separated	2 teaspoons cold soy sauce
½ cup flour or rice flour	½ teaspoon salt
½ cup ice-cold beer	½ teaspoon dry mustard
2 teaspoons cold olive oil	¼ teaspoon white pepper

The Dipping Sauce

½ cup Japanese soy sauce	1 tablespoon brown sugar
2 tablespoons sake or dry vermouth	1 teaspoon finely grated fresh gingerroot
1 tablespoon rice vinegar	½ teaspoon black pepper

Behead, peel, and devein the shrimp, leaving the tails on. Rig for deep frying, heating several inches of oil to 375 degrees. While you wait for the oil to heat, mix all the batter ingredients except the egg whites in a chilled bowl, whisking together thoroughly. In a smaller bowl, beat the egg whites until stiff, then fold carefully and gently into the batter. The idea is to avoid losing the air in the egg whites. Do not combine too vigorously; leave perhaps a streak or two of egg white. Holding a shrimp by the tail, dip it into a bowl of flour, then into the batter. Let the shrimp drip over the batter for a few seconds, then put it gently into the hot oil. Repeat until you have six to eight shrimp in the hot oil. Do not overcrowd. Fry until the batter is crisp and golden—3 or 4 minutes, depending on the size of the shrimp. If all has gone well, the shrimp will have fluffed up. Drain carefully on paper towels or a brown bag while you cook another batch. It's best to have the paper towels or brown bag on a hot platter, or to put them in a slow oven, to keep them very warm. If they're allowed to cool, the shrimp tend to become soggy. Serve on heated plates, along with the dipping sauce. Feeds 2 or more.

Fried go-withs: The Japanese also dip fresh vegetables into the tempura batter and and fry them in the oil, serving them with the shrimp. Try fresh mushrooms, asparagus, green beans, sliced sweet potatoes, lotus root, sliced squash, sliced green tomatoes, and so on, all dipped into the tempura batter and deep fried.

SHRIMP CAKES

The Vietnamese offer us some unexpected ways with shrimp, and this is one. I have adapted the recipe from *The Classic Cuisine of Vietnam*, by Bach Ngo and Gloria Zimmerman, a book that I highly recommend.

1½ pounds beheaded raw shrimp, medium (2 pounds heads-on shrimp)	1½ cups water
	1 medium to large potato
2 to 3 cups peanut oil	salt and freshly ground black pepper to taste
1½ cups all-purpose flour	Nuoc Cham sauce (page 177)

1. Shuck the shrimp, saving the heads, peelings, and tails for Shrimp Stock (page 181), if needed for another recipe. Mash half the shrimp into a paste in your mortar and pestle. Cut the rest in half lengthwise. Set aside.

2. Peel the potato and cut into very thin slices, as when making potato chips. Then cut the slices into thin strips. Set aside.

3. Mix the flour and water in a suitable bowl, stirring until smooth. Add the shrimp paste, salt, and pepper to the batter, then stir in the potato strings.

4. In a suitable pot, heat the oil to 375 degrees. Using a shallow rounded ladle, scoop up about 2 tablespoons of the batter. Place a shrimp half into the ladle. Drop the batter and shrimp half into the hot oil. Fry for about 3 minutes, turning a time or two, or until golden brown. Drain. Serve hot or cold, with Nuoc Cham sauce, of course. Feeds 2 or more.

Note: The Vietnamese sometimes use whole small shrimp in the batter, then eat them shell and all. Try this if you feel culinarily adventurous and have kindred guests.

FINGER-LICKING SHRIMP

If you've got the right company to feed, this recipe provides some good sensuous eating.

beheaded fresh shrimp or heads-on shrimp, large (fully shucked shrimp just won't do)	olive oil for deep frying (at least ½ gallon) freshly ground sea salt and black pepper

Rig for deep frying at 375 degrees, heating at least 3 inches of olive oil in a suitable pot. (The propane- or butane-fueled fish fryers work nicely.) When the oil is right, drop a few of the shrimp into it. Cook for about 3 minutes, until nicely pink. Remove and drain on a brown bag. Cook the rest of the shrimp and grind some sea salt and black pepper over them. Serve hot. When you peel the shrimp at the table, the salt and pepper and olive oil coat the fingers for the licking. Servings? I allow ¾ pound of beheaded shrimp per person.

7

Shrimp in
the Skillet

A good skillet comes in handy for frying or sautéing a
small amount of shrimp, usually for 1 to 3 people. For
larger fries, a deeper pot partly filled with several inches of oil works better simply because it permits the cook to fry
more shrimp at a time. Any good heavy-duty skillet will do for
shrimp; cast iron is my personal favorite. A large electric skillet
also comes in handy from time to time, especially for cooking
such multi-ingredient dishes as shrimp chow mein.

A cast-iron skillet may be even better than a wok for stir-
frying shrimp, but the few stir-fry recipes in this chapter can
also be cooked in a wok, covered in more detail in chapter 8.

A. D.'S SKILLET FRY

I love to fry fish fillets and chicken fingers in a cast-iron skillet
with enough oil to only half cover the pieces—and shrimp fit

right in with this scheme. The idea is to have the bottom of the shrimp in direct contact with the skillet, with oil on the sides. With medium shrimp, about ½ inch of oil will do the trick. Usually, I cook this one only for 2 people. If more people are sitting in, deep frying is much quicker and doesn't require that the shrimp be turned. For this recipe, I allow only freshly ground fine white cornmeal. The gritty yellow supermarket meals won't stick to the shrimp without using egg or a flour batter. Apart from the great flavor and texture it imparts, skillet frying also reduces the fat content because the coating doesn't soak up lots of oil.

1½ pounds beheaded raw shrimp,　　**peanut oil**
**　　medium to large (2 pounds**　　**salt**
**　　heads-on shrimp)**　　**cayenne pepper (optional)**
fresh stone-ground fine
**　　white cornmeal**

Peel the shrimp, leaving the tails intact. Save the heads and shells for stock, if needed for another recipe. Sprinkle the shrimp lightly with salt and cayenne (if you like), then coat with cornmeal. The latter is easily accomplished by putting a little meal in a small bag and shaking a few shrimp at a time. Heat the oil to 350 degrees. Fry the shrimp a few at a time for about 4 minutes, turning once. Drain and serve hot.

These can be served with hush puppies and a large salad, or with vegetables of your choice. For a cookout, try serving these (along with french fries) in a newspaper rolled into a cone, like British fish-and-chips. Having the tail for use as a handle makes these easy to eat.

SHRIMP AND GRAVY

Here's a versatile dish that can be served at any time, including breakfast (with scrambled chicken eggs and hot biscuit halves), lunch (with a tossed salad, corn on the cob, and a crusty bread), for supper (served over rice). Part of the plan is to sop up the gravy with the bread, or to serve it over biscuit halves or rice.

1½ pounds beheaded fresh shrimp, medium (2 pounds heads-on shrimp)
4 slices smoked bacon or salt pork

¼ cup all-purpose flour
salt and freshly ground black pepper
boiling water

Shuck the shrimp, deveining if you must. Save the heads, tails, and peelings for stock (page 181) if wanted for another recipe; set the meats aside. Fry the bacon in a cast-iron skillet. Drain the bacon and keep it warm. Add the shrimp to the drippings in the skillet and fry over medium heat for 3 minutes. Stir in the flour. Slowly stir in some boiling water, using enough to make a thin gravy. Sprinkle with salt and pepper. Simmer—but do not hard boil—for about 20 minutes, stirring frequently. Serve with bread or hot biscuit halves and the cooked bacon. Feeds 2 to 4.

SHRIMP SAUTÉED IN BUTTER

Don't let the simplicity of this dish fool you. It's very good, if you've got really fresh shrimp. It's best prepared in a large skillet or electric skillet, with some emphasis on *large*, so that the shrimp won't overlap each other very much.

1½ pounds beheaded raw
  shrimp, medium or large
  (2 pounds heads-on shrimp)
½ cup butter
1 medium to large onion,
  chopped

1 tablespoon freshly squeezed
  lemon juice
chopped fresh parsley
salt and freshly ground
  black pepper
rice (cooked separately)

Behead, peel, and devein the shrimp, saving the trimmings for
stock (page 181) if wanted for another recipe. Sauté the onion
in the butter for a few minutes. Add the shrimp meats and
lemon juice. Cook for 4 or 5 minutes, turning with a wooden
spoon, until the shrimp turn nicely pink. Sprinkle with salt, pepper, and parsley. Serve hot over a bed of rice. Feeds 2 to 4.

SHRIMP SCAMPI

This old Italian dish is sometimes made with a small member of
the lobster family, or scampi, similar to the *langoustine*. These
days it's more often made with shrimp, and in recipes and cookbooks we even see "chicken scampi" listed. My take is that it's
simply a sauté in butter or olive oil, similar to the recipe above
with the addition of plenty of garlic. More and more we are seeing it served on pasta.

1½ pounds beheaded raw
  shrimp, large (2 pounds
  heads-on shrimp)
¼ cup butter
¼ cup dry white wine

8 cloves garlic, chopped
juice of ½ lemon
1 chicken egg, whisked
salt and freshly ground
  black pepper

Shuck and devein the shrimp, saving the heads, tails, and shells
for stock (page 181), if needed for another recipe. In a skillet,
heat the butter and sauté the garlic for 4 or 5 minutes, stirring

with a wooden spoon. Dip the shrimp into the whisked egg, coating all sides, and drop them into the skillet. Sauté for 4 or 5 minutes, or until the shrimp turn pink. Add the wine and lemon juice, along with some salt and pepper. Cook for another 2 minutes, stirring a time or two, and serve hot with rice or pasta, along with a salad, hot Italian bread, and vino. Feeds 2 or more.

Greek variation: Use olive oil instead of butter and add the zest of the lemon along with the juice. Serve with grilled eggplant.

LEFTOVER-SHRIMP SAUTÉ

Here's an easy Cajun dish. It calls for Cajun fish spice, which is a commercial mix developed for blackening redfish. Several brands are marketed, and you should be able to find one in most large supermarkets or by mail order. Although the ingredients list calls for cooked shrimp (possibly leftovers from a boil), you can also use freshly peeled shrimp to advantage. Just sauté them a little longer, putting them in with the green onion.

1 pound cooked shrimp tails
½ cup butter
1 cup chopped green onions
    with part of green tops
1 tablespoon white wine
    Worcestershire sauce

1 teaspoon Cajun seafood
    seasoning (or to taste)
salt to taste
rice (cooked separately)

Melt the butter in a cast-iron skillet. Sauté the onions for 4 or 5 minutes, then stir in the Cajun seasoning, salt, and white wine Worcestershire sauce. Toss in the cooked shrimp and stir until quite hot. Serve over rice. Feeds 2 or more if you've got plenty of rice.

THAI SHRIMP IN FISH SAUCE

I'm very fond of Thai and Vietnamese fish sauce, using it as a table condiment as well as an ingredient in recipes, and my dog Nosher thinks that a generous sprinkling of the stuff can turn ordinary Gravy Train into gourmet dog chow. Note that fish sauce is very salty, so no extra salt is added to the recipe. The Thai cook this dish with the aid of a brown syrup made of caramelized sugar along with some regular granulated sugar. I cook it with dark brown sugar substituting for both. If you're a stickler for the real thing, see *The Classic Cuisine of Vietnam*, by Bach Ngo and Gloria Zimmerman.

¾ **pound beheaded raw shrimp,** **medium to small (1 pound** **heads-on shrimp)**	**2 tablespoons dark brown sugar** **1 tablespoon peanut oil** **1 clove garlic, minced**
3 tablespoons Thai fish sauce	**freshly ground black pepper**

Behead and shuck the shrimp, removing the tail fin. Devein if you must. Heat the peanut oil in a wok or skillet over high heat. Add the garlic, stir a time or two with a wooden spoon, and add the shrimp. Reduce the heat to medium. Stirring as you go, add the fish sauce, sugar, and black pepper. Cover and simmer for 3 or 4 minutes. Serve with rice and a Thai vegetable platter. Feeds 2 at my house. Typically, the Thai, who usually eat only small portions of meat or fish, might well make 4 servings of this dish. It's very filling, owing partly to the richness of the fish sauce.

SHRIMP CHOW MEIN

This dish is best cooked in a large skillet, and a square 12- or 13-inch electric skillet is perfect. You'll also need a pot for boiling the shrimp.

1½ pounds beheaded raw
  shrimp, medium (2 pounds
  heads-on shrimp)
2 cups mung bean sprouts
2 cups sliced mushrooms
1 cup shredded bok choy
1 cup halved snow pea pods
2 stalks celery with tops,
  chopped
1 medium to large onion,
  sliced lengthwise
3 cloves garlic, minced

½ red bell pepper, finely chopped
½ cup sliced water chestnuts
½ cup slivered almonds, toasted
¼ cup peanut oil
¼ cup soy sauce
2 tablespoons cornstarch
salt and freshly ground
  black pepper to taste
chow mein noodles
more soy sauce to taste
salted water

1. Boil the shrimp in salted water for 2 or 3 minutes, or until they turn nicely pink. Remove the shrimp with a strainer (leaving the liquid in the pot) and drain until cool enough to handle. Dress the shrimp, cutting each one in half lengthwise and putting the heads, tails, and peelings back into the pot, along with the celery. Set the dressed shrimp aside. Simmer the peelings and heads in the pot for 30 minutes or so. Strain the stock, discarding the solids. Measure out 1½ cups of stock, adding a little water if needed. Mix ¼ cup of the stock with the cornstarch. Set aside and keep the remaining 1¼ cups of the stock hot.

2. In a large skillet (or electric skillet), heat the peanut oil and sauté the shrimp for about 1½ minutes. Remove the shrimp with a hand strainer.

3. Sauté for 2 or 3 minutes the onion, garlic, bean sprouts, mushrooms, bok choy, red bell pepper, snow pea pods, and water chestnuts, stirring with a wooden spoon. Add the reserved shrimp stock, soy sauce, salt, and pepper. Simmer, covered, for 8 to 10 minutes.

4. Stir the cornstarch mixture into the skillet contents, and add the shrimp. Cook, stirring as you go, until the mixture starts to bubble. Stir in the almonds. Serve over chow mein noodles, with more soy sauce on the side. Feeds 4 to 6.

SKILLET SHRIMP ÉTOUFFÉE

This dish can be cooked in a large skillet or in a stovetop Dutch oven. An electric skillet is perfect.

2¼ pound beheaded raw shrimp, medium (3 pounds heads-on shrimp)
¼ cup butter
¼ cup finely chopped celery with tops
¼ cup finely chopped green onions with part of tops
2 cloves garlic, minced
2 tablespoons chopped fresh parsley
2 tablespoons flour
2 bay leaves
salt and cayenne pepper to taste
rice (cooked separately)
water

1. Dress the shrimp, putting the heads, tails, and peelings into a pot of boiling water, along with the bay leaves. (Devein the shrimp, if you must.) Set the shrimp aside. Cover the pot and simmer for 30 minutes or so. Strain out 1 cup of the stock and set aside. Save the rest of the stock, if needed for another recipe, or discard it along with the solids.

2. Heat the butter in a skillet. Stir in the flour with a wooden spoon and keep stirring for 5 minutes or longer. Add the onion, garlic, and celery; cook for 5 minutes.

3. Add the reserved shrimp stock, parsley, salt, and cayenne. Bring to a boil. Add the shrimp and simmer for 3 or 4 minutes, or until they turn nicely pink. Serve over a bed of rice. Feeds 3 or more.

BILL'S STIR-FRY

My son Bill gave me this recipe, saying that he wrote it on a napkin after eating a similar dish in a restaurant. Any good spicy sausage will do, but I like a pork link with some fat, which helps flavor the whole.

¾ pound beheaded fresh
   shrimp, large (1 pound
   heads-on shrimp)
¼ pound spicy pork sausage
½ green bell pepper, seeded
½ red bell pepper, seeded
½ large onion, peeled and
   cut in half lengthwise

1 portabella mushroom
1 tablespoon chopped parsley
olive oil (if needed)
salt and black pepper
   (if needed)
rice (cooked separately)

Cut the sausage diagonally into ovals about ½ inch thick. Dress the shrimp (saving the heads and tails for stock if needed for another recipe), and set aside. Cut all the vegetables into strips suitable for a stir-fry and set aside. Fry the sausage in a cast-iron skillet for about 2 minutes on each side. (If the sausage is fatty, it will need no oil; if not, add a little olive oil to the skillet.) Drain the sausage. Stir-fry the shrimp in the skillet for 2 minutes. Set aside. Stir-fry the vegetables and parsley for 4 or 5 minutes. Add the sausage and shrimp back to the skillet, along with a little water. Cover and cook for 4 or 5 minutes. Serve hot over rice. Feeds 2 to 4.

SHRIMP CREOLE

Tomatoes, onions, and peppers characterize Creole cookery, and the best of these dishes is Shrimp Creole. The measures below work well for a large skillet or perhaps a stovetop Dutch oven. An electric skillet will do, but cast iron is better. Some cooks insist on peeling and seeding the tomatoes, but I don't bother unless I'm cooking for French guests.

3 pounds beheaded raw
   shrimp, medium (4 pounds
   heads-on shrimp)
½ cup butter or margarine
3 medium tomatoes, chopped
1 large onion, chopped
4 cloves garlic, minced
½ red bell pepper, minced
½ green bell pepper, minced

2 jalapeños, seeded and minced
1 tablespoon minced
   fresh thyme
salt and freshly ground
   black pepper
rice (cooked separately)
Shrimp Stock (page 181),
   water, or chicken stock

Dress the shrimp, deveining if you prefer. Make a stock with the heads, tails, and peelings (page 181). Reserve ½ cup or so of the stock, saving the rest for another recipe. (If you're in a hurry, substitute water or chicken stock.) Heat the butter in a skillet. Sauté the onion and all the peppers for about 5 minutes, stirring with a wooden spoon. Add the garlic and thyme, stirring for a minute or so. Add the tomatoes and the reserved Shrimp Stock. Bring to a boil. Add the shrimp, bring quickly to a new boil, and cook for 3 minutes. Stir in salt and pepper to taste. Let sit for a few minutes. Serve hot over rice. Feeds 4 to 6.

BURMESE TIGER PRAWNS

I include this traditional dish from Burma not only because it's so good but also to strengthen my case for marketing fresh shrimp with their heads intact. The recipe has been adapted here from *The Burmese Kitchen,* by Copeland Marks, who says it "really requires the head oil to give it the full seasoning." A tiger prawn is simply a large shrimp with dark stripes. Any large or jumbo shrimp can be substituted. Marks says that 1 pound of these shrimp serves 4 people. I can get by with this, if I've got plenty of rice and vegetables and bread—but I really do want more shrimp. Consequently, I have increased the measures in the recipe. Note that the colors of the cooked shrimp flesh, head oil, and turmeric combine to give the dish an orange hue.

2 pounds heads-on raw shrimp, large (1½ pounds beheaded shrimp)	**4 cloves garlic, thinly sliced**
	1 teaspoon salt
	¼ teaspoon ground turmeric
2 tablespoons peanut oil	**2 tablespoons water**

Pull the heads off the shrimp and scoop out the fat, perhaps using a baby spoon. Shuck and tail the shrimp. Add the shrimp-head fat, salt, and turmeric to the shrimp, mixing well. Heat the oil in a skillet and fry the garlic until it turns yellow, stirring with a wooden spoon. Add the shrimp and stir-fry for 2 minutes. Add the water and cook for another 2 minutes, stirring as you go, or until the water evaporates. Serve warm with rice and vegetables or other dishes.

SHRIMP MOSCA, MY WAY

Some of the best of New Orleans cookery is of Italian influence—as in this recipe, which calls for lots of garlic and olive oil. The shrimp are, of course, cooked whole and eaten at the table. In my version of this recipe, however, I pull the heads off the shrimp and cook them in oil for a few minutes in order to incorporate the head fat into the sauce. The original recipe was created by Chef Nick Mosca of Elmwood Plantation, I understand, and he specified headless shrimp in the shell. He also cooked his shrimp for about 30 minutes, total. I prefer mine cooked for a shorter time, adding them toward the end. Suit yourself.

2 pounds heads-on shrimp, jumbo (or use 1½ pounds beheaded raw shrimp and forget about the head oil)	**1 teaspoon salt**
½ cup olive oil	**1 teaspoon crushed black pepper**
¼ cup Sauternes	**1 teaspoon dried rosemary**
24 cloves garlic, peeled	**1 teaspoon dried oregano**
2 bay leaves	**lemon wedges (for garnish)**
	freshly snipped parsley (for garnish)

Twist the head off each shrimp, leaving the body in its shell with the tail attached. With a small spoon, remove the head fat and set it aside. Heat the olive oil in a large cast-iron skillet. Add the head fat. Sauté the garlic for a few minutes then add the wine, bay leaves, oregano, salt, pepper, and rosemary. Cook over medium heat for about 20 minutes, stirring as you go to incorporate all the flavors. Discard the bay leaves. Increase the heat to high. Add the shrimp, cover, and cook for 5 or 6 minutes, or until the shrimp are nicely pink. Serve in bowls and ladle in some of the pan juice, garnishing with a lemon wedge and a sprig of parsley. Serve with hot Italian bread for dunking, along with a colorful tossed salad and perhaps some vino. Feeds 2 or more.

Note: There are many variations of this dish, and some people use a commercial Mosca sauce to make it. (See chapter 16.)

BAHAMIAN SHRIMP

Brazilians love their shrimp, and some big ones grow in the Bahamian region. The coconut milk used in the recipe is available canned in Asian and Latin markets. Do not use the coconut "water" inside the shell. Most good cooks will want to peel and chop the tomatoes, but I seldom go that far. Suit yourself.

1½ pounds beheaded raw
  shrimp, large or jumbo
  (2 pounds heads-on shrimp)
1½ cups coconut milk
⅓ cup fresh lime juice or
  lemon juice
¼ cup olive oil
3 medium tomatoes, chopped

3 spring onions, minced with
  most of the green tops
1 large onion, minced
3 cloves garlic, minced
salt and freshly ground
  black pepper
water

Behead and shuck the shrimp, putting the heads, shells, and tails into a pot. Devein the shrimp (if you must) and put the meats into a bowl. Add the lime juice, garlic, salt, and pepper. Toss to mix well and set aside. To the pot with the shrimp heads, tails, and shells, add 3 cups of water. Bring to a boil and simmer for 30 minutes. Strain and discard the solids. Reduce the strained stock to ¾ cup. Set aside. Heat the olive oil in a skillet. Sauté the onions and spring onions for 3 or 4 minutes. Add the shrimp stock and tomatoes. Simmer for 5 minutes, or until the mixture thickens. Stir in the coconut milk and shrimp. Cook for 3 or 4 minutes, or until the shrimp are nicely pink, turning a time or two. Add a little salt and pepper to taste. Serve over fluffy white rice. Servings? I allow ¾ pound of beheaded shrimp per person, but most books recommend less. So make do if you must.

8

Shrimp in the Wok

A sian cookery has become increasingly popular in America during the past few decades, owing partly to the wok and the stir-fry technique. Often recipes for the wok can be cooked in a good skillet, preferably cast iron; conversely, the wok can be used for many skillet dishes as well as for deep frying. In a pinch the wok will do even for boiling shrimp, and it works nicely for steamed shrimp when fitted with a bamboo steamer.

A large steel wok is recommended, and I also like the flat-bottomed cast-iron woks for cooking on a gas stove. Some of the Teflon or other woks with nonstick coatings are not suitable for use over high heat.

Here are a few recipes for cooking shrimp in a wok.

HONG KONG SHRIMP

When you make the shrimp stock in the wok for this recipe, consider steaming the vegetables at the same time if you've got a bamboo steamer that fits on top.

1½ pounds beheaded raw
  shrimp, medium (2 pounds
  heads-on shrimp)
¼ pound minced fresh pork loin
2 tablespoons oyster sauce
2 tablespoons peanut oil
  (maybe more)
1 tablespoon soy sauce
1 tablespoon rice wine or
  dry vermouth
1 tablespoon minced (or
  finely julienned) fresh
  gingerroot

1 tablespoon fermented black
  beans (available in Asian
  markets)
3 green onions with tops,
  chopped
3 cloves garlic, minced
1 rib celery with green
  tops, chopped
1 chicken egg, whisked
1 teaspoon cornstarch
¼ teaspoon brown sugar
water (or chicken stock)
salt

1. Dress the shrimp, putting the heads, tails, and peelings into a wok or stockpot. Cover well with water, add a little salt and the chopped celery, bring to a boil, cover, and simmer for 30 minutes or so, adding more water if needed. Strain the stock, discarding the solids. Measure out ½ cup of the stock for this recipe and keep it handy. Bottle the rest for use another day. If you want to bypass this step, substitute ½ cup of chicken stock. Dry the wok, getting it ready for stir-frying.

2. While the stock is simmering, marinate the shrimp in the soy sauce and rice wine for 15 or 20 minutes, tossing about from time to time.

3. With a mortar and pestle, mash together the fermented black beans and garlic, making a thick paste. Keep it handy.

4. Get all the other ingredients measured out and ready in small containers so that you'll have everything at hand.

5. Heat the wok and add the oil. Drain the shrimp and pat dry with paper towels. Set the marinade aside. Stir-fry the shrimp for 2 or 3 minutes, until nicely pink. Remove with a hand strainer and drain.

6. Stir-fry the pork for 2 or 3 minutes. Remove and drain.

7. In the remaining oil, stir-fry the green onions and ginger for 5 minutes, using a little more peanut oil if necessary. Stir in the black bean sauce, oyster sauce, sugar, and remaining marinade, simmering for 3 or 4 minutes. Add the shrimp stock (or chicken stock). Add the cooked pork, shrimp, and cornstarch. Cook and stir for a minute or so, then slowly add the whisked egg, stirring as you go. Serve hot with rice and steamed vegetables. Feeds 2 or more.

CENTRAL VIETNAMESE SHRIMP AND PORK

Pork is very popular in Vietnam, and shrimp are plentiful in the waters. This recipe combines these favorites, and is eaten with a specialty known as shrimp chips. Raw shrimp chips can be purchased in some markets that traffic in the authentic fare of Southeast Asia. These must be fried before serving. This recipe has been adapted from *The Classic Cuisine of Vietnam,* by Bach Ngo and Gloria Zimmerman, which says it is from the central part of that country. I have taken the liberty to double the measures of both pork and shrimp.

¾ **pound beheaded raw shrimp, medium to large (1 pound heads-on shrimp)**
½ **pound fresh pork, thinly sliced**
1 **can bamboo shoots (5-ounce size)**
¼ **cup roasted peanuts**
2 **tablespoons toasted sesame seeds**

1½ **tablespoons peanut oil**
2 **shallots, chopped**
1 **clove garlic, chopped**
1 **tablespoon chopped fresh mint leaves**
1 **tablespoon fish sauce**
black pepper to taste
Fried Shrimp Chips (page 153)

1. Shuck the shrimp, saving the heads, tails, and peelings for stock, if wanted for another recipe (page 181). Cut the shrimp in half, then cut into strips. Slice the bamboo shoots into strips ⅛ inch thick and ¼ inch wide.

2. Heat the wok and add the peanut oil. Stir-fry the shallots and garlic for a minute or so. Add the pork. Stir-fry for 2 minutes, or until lightly browned. Add the shrimp and stir-fry for 2 minutes.

3. Add the bamboo shoots, fish sauce, and black pepper, mixing well. Add the peanuts, sesame seeds, and mint leaves. Toss and remove the wok from the heat. Add the contents to a serving platter.

4. Serve hot or at room temperature, along with shrimp chips. (If you don't have Fried Shrimp Chips, use thin crackers.) Use the chips to dip up the mixture, helped along with a chopstick. These measures will serve 6 to 8 people as a first course. I like it as a main coarse or light lunch, for which it will feed 2 to 4.

HEADHUNTER SHRIMP

Here's a Malayan shrimp dish, adapted from *Dining with Headhunters,* by Richard Sterling. Sterling says the recipe (which he calls Chile Prawns) denotes a style or broad approach, like the term *gumbo.*

¾ **pound beheaded raw shrimp, jumbo (1 pound heads-on shrimp)**	1 **tablespoon cayenne pepper**
	1 **tablespoon ground coriander (cilantro seeds)**
1 **cup water**	2 **teaspoons freshly ground black pepper**
¼ **cup peanut oil**	
1 **small to medium onion, grated**	1 **teaspoon ground lemongrass**
	½ **teaspoon salt**

Mix the last five ingredients and the water. Put the shrimp into a nonmetallic container, pour in the spice mixture, and toss to coat all sides of the shrimp. Marinate for 10 minutes. Drain the shrimp, retaining the marinade. Heat the oil in a wok and stir-fry the onion for 2 minutes or so. Add the shrimp. Stir-fry for about 5 minutes, or until the shrimp turn bright pink. Put the shrimp on a heated platter and keep warm. Put the reserved marinade into the wok, increase the heat to high, and reduce the marinade until you have a thick dipping sauce. Serve the shrimp warm, along with the sauce. Feeds 2, Sterling says—but I can eat the whole batch. Note that these shrimp are quite hot, owing to the cayenne and black pepper. Note also that they're even hotter if you use shrimp with the heads pinched off—or shucked—because more of the meat is exposed directly to the spices.

CHEF MYRON'S VELVETED SHRIMP

Chef Myron Becker, a culinary sport who brews and bottles Myron's 20-Gauge Wild Game Sauce and several exceptional Asian sauces for the gourmet trade, gave me this version of a classic Chinese shrimp dish. It goes best with his Chef Myron's Ponzu Sauce. If you can't find it, Becker says, try the following creation, using, he emphasizes, a high-quality aged shoyu sauce (a Japanese soy sauce).

THE PONZU SAUCE

½ cup long-aged shoyu

3 tablespoons sake

3 tablespoons lime juice

2 tablespoons honey

1 tablespoon rice wine vinegar

1 tablespoon minced
   fresh gingerroot

½ teaspoon minced fresh garlic

roasted sesame oil

Put all the sauce ingredients except the sesame oil into a saucepan, bring to a simmer, and continue simmering for a few minutes. Cool and stir in a few drops of roasted sesame oil. (The sesame cooking oil won't do.) Set aside.

THE SHRIMP

1½ pounds beheaded raw white Gulf shrimp, medium (2 pounds heads-on shrimp)

Ponzu Sauce (above)
egg white
cornstarch
½ cup peanut oil

Shuck and butterfly the shrimp. Put them into a nonmetallic container. Add 3 tablespoons of Ponzu Sauce and a little egg white. Marinate for 15 minutes or so. Sprinkle lightly with cornstarch, stirring about and kneading with your fingers until the shrimp take on a smooth and slightly slimy feeling. Heat the peanut oil almost to the smoke point in a wok. Stir-fry quickly but gently, turning to keep the shrimp separated in the oil, for about 2 minutes, until they're very lightly golden. Do not overcook. The shrimp will stick to paper towels, so drain them in a sieve. Serve in a bowl, garnished with scallions or cilantro, with a separate bowl for the Ponzu Sauce. Feeds 2 or more.

9

Shrimp on the Skewer

Everybody loves the kabob, a method of cooking in which cubes of meat or chunks of vegetables or fruit are strung together on a stick or long skewer. The stick holds the food for cooking and usually for serving. Each diner gets a whole kabob, often served atop a bed of rice or pilaf.

Some kinds of skewers work better than others for shrimp. Here's my take, hopefully with a surprise or two.

BAMBOO SKEWERS

Inexpensive, more or less disposable, and widely available in modern supermarkets and specialty shops, these are my favorite for shrimp. Typically they're 10 or 12 inches long and tapered from the middle toward either end. Most kabob authorities suggest that bamboo skewers be soaked overnight in water before use, but I confess that I sometimes don't do this.

METAL RODS

These conventional skewers, often with a fancy handle, work fine for shrimp. In a pinch you can make them simply by cutting the crosspieces out of an old rack from a kitchen stove or grill. When using any kind of wire, such as from refrigerators or coat hangers, make sure it will take the heat. Some wire coatings won't stand up to high heat and may contaminate the food.

FLAT METAL SKEWERS

These sword-shaped skewers, usually made of thin metal, are better suited for larger kabobs made from beef or lamb. They're widely used in the Middle East and are perfect for holding kabobs fashioned from ground meats. When you're using ground shrimp, it's best to shape the kabob around the blade.

RAILROAD SKEWERS

To keep shrimp from rotating on the skewer during the cooking process, they can be strung up on two parallel skewers. Picture a railroad track. The rails are the two skewers; the cross ties, the shrimp. Bamboo skewers are ideal for railroading. When loading the shrimp, it's best to alternate heads and tails, snugging the shrimp up tightly.

FLAVORING SKEWERS

In Asia kabobs are sometimes shaped around sticks of lemongrass or other flavoring stalks. (See the recipe for Balinese Kabobs on page 109.) Short kabobs can be made by splitting the core of a pineapple. If you're adventurous, you might want to try aromatic woods. I have, for example, cooked kabobs in camp on sticks from the sassafras tree.

Short Skewers

Sometimes short skewers are used for holding a piece of bacon around the meat, and for use as a handle while cooking on a grill. Round toothpicks work, but the thin flat toothpicks are a little too flimsy for use.

In Vietnam and other parts of Asia, crab claws are sometimes used (after the meat has been eaten off them) as short skewers on which to mold ground-shrimp kabobs.

Shrimp kabobs are usually cooked by grilling or broiling, but they can also be baked or even fried. In addition to the suggestions below, many of the recipes in other chapters of this book can easily be adapted for kabob cookery. Recipes for grilling or broiling shrimp will often work with kabobs.

CAJUN KABOBS

Here's one of my favorites. Somewhat surprisingly, these kabobs aren't sprinkled liberally with Cajun dust of any sort. Instead, the flavors come through from the andouille sausage. To make sure that the sausage is done, I like to poach it separately, then slice it for the kabobs.

beheaded or heads-on raw shrimp, jumbo	long-grain white rice (cooked separately)
smoked andouille sausage	tossed salad (fixed separately)

In an electric skillet or other suitable pan, simmer the sausage in a little water (tightly covered) for about 10 minutes, cooking it through; keep it hot. Rig for grilling over charcoal or wood coals, placing the rack about 4 inches over the heat. Dress the shrimp, possibly saving the head and peelings for making stock for another day (page 181). Slice the sausage on a diagonal, from ½ to ¾ inch thick. Skewer the shrimp and sausage, beginning and ending with shrimp. Grill for 2 or 3 minutes, turn, and grill for another 2 or 3 minutes. Serve hot over a bed of rice, along with a large bowl of tossed salad and crusty bread. I allow ¾ pound of beheaded shrimp per person.

FLAT-SKEWER SHRIMP KABOBS

In the Middle East ground lamb and other meats are shaped around a long, thin skewer and grilled like kabobs. This scheme works nicely with shrimp, although flat skewers may be difficult to locate. I have only a part of a set, originally from Iran. Two small bamboo skewers work pretty well, but it's best to rig for grilling without a rack. I do this by spacing 12 bricks in two parallel rows, stacked 2 high and 3 long, with hot coals in the center. Then the skewers can be placed across the coals without having to rest the meat or shrimp on a metal grill or rack; this rig precludes sticking and makes it easier to keep the kabobs intact while you're turning them and removing them from the fire. Charcoal works fine, but wood coals are also good. In either case, build the fire away from the kabob rig, then transfer the hot coals with a garden scoop.

3 pounds beheaded raw shrimp, medium (4 pounds heads-on raw shrimp)
2 medium onions, chopped
1 red bell pepper, chopped
¼ cup chopped fresh parsley or cilantro
2 tablespoons chili powder
olive oil
salt

Shuck the shrimp, saving the heads, tails, and peelings for stock (page 181) if desired. Set the shrimp aside and rig for grilling, as directed above. While the coals get hot, heat a little olive oil in a skillet and sauté the onions and bell pepper for 5 minutes or so; set aside. Grind the shrimp in a sausage mill using a ⁳⁄₁₆-inch wheel, or chop them rather finely. (Be careful with food processors; you don't need mushy shrimp.) Using your hands, mix all the ingredients and form the mixture around skewers, making sausagelike shapes about 1 inch in diameter and about 6 inches long. Place the kabobs over the hot coals, resting the ends of the skewers on the bricks. Grill for 4 or 5 minutes on each side. Do not overcook. Serve hot on a bed of rice or pilaf along with grilled eggplant or vegetables and green stuff of your choice. Serves 4 or more.

BALINESE KABOBS

Here's a seafood kabob with welcome but perhaps unfamiliar flavors. In Bali the kabob, or satay, is cooked over a fire made of coconut husks. A hardwood or charcoal fire will do, burned down to coals. Part of the flavor of this satay comes from the lemongrass skewers. Fresh lemongrass is available in some supermarkets these days, but use bamboo skewers if you must. The fish used in the recipe can be any firm white fillets.

1 pound peeled raw shrimp, medium*
1 pound boneless fish fillets
3 cups grated fresh coconut
¾ cup Bali Seafood Paste (page 167)
7 or 8 fresh lime leaves, shredded

3 tablespoons light brown sugar
¾ tablespoon salt
½ tablespoon freshly ground black pepper
4 to 8 green bird's-eye chili peppers (be careful)
lemongrass stalks, cut into 6-inch skewers

Be warned: Balinese bird's-eye peppers make a very hot dish. These tiny peppers are pure fire, and they can burn your skin. Be very careful when seeding them. If you don't want extremely hot food, use a jalapeño or two, or other hot peppers such as cayennes. Finely mince the fish and shrimp. (A food processor can be used.) Thoroughly mix in all the other ingredients except the lemongrass. Shape the mixture around the lemongrass skewers, using a heaping tablespoon for each. Grill over hot coals until golden brown, turning once. The very bottom of both sides should be slightly charred, owing partly to the caramelized sugar. It's the Balinese way. Serve as finger food, or as a meal with coconut rice, steamed yard-long beans (or fiddleheads), and fried bananas. Feeds 3 or 4, or more.

Note: Rice is essential for a Balinese meal, and it is cooked in several ways, often with pandan or salam leaves. To make an easy coconut rice, simply cook long-grain white rice in coconut milk instead of in water.

*Start with 1½ pounds of beheaded shrimp or 2 pounds of heads-on raw shrimp.

VIETNAMESE SUGARCANE SHRIMP

This traditional shrimp dish can be made by following any of several published recipes. I consider this one to be authentic. To make it, you'll need a length of sugarcane, which grows in great plenty if Vietnam and in some southern parts of the United States. It's used for making sugar, and locals like it for making cane juice and syrup—and for chewing. If you have access to fresh sugarcane, peel a stalk and cut out four of the joints, leaving three round pieces 4 to 6 inches long. Cut each round into quarters, giving you 12 sticks. If you can't obtain fresh sugarcane at a reasonable price, try quartering the core

SHRIMP ON THE SKEWER

of a pineapple or using segments of lemongrass (see the Balinese recipe above). Also note that crab claws (after the meat has been eaten) are traditionally used in Vietnam for the same purpose.

¾ to 1 pound beheaded raw
   shrimp, medium (1½ to 2
   pounds heads-on shrimp)
3 segments sugarcane, prepared
   as instructed above
2 tablespoons pork fat
2 chicken egg whites,
   whisked until frothy

4 cloves garlic
1½ tablespoons rice
1 teaspoon sugar
black pepper to taste
peanut oil

1. Behead, tail, and shuck the shrimp, saving the trimmings for stock, if wanted (page 181). Devein the shrimp if you prefer. Set aside.

2. Prepare the sugarcane sticks as directed above, or prepare a suitable substitute. You'll need 12 sticks of some sort. Set aside.

3. Heat the rice in a small skillet until it browns. Grind the rice to a powder in a small mortar and pestle. Set aside.

4. Boil the pork fat in water for about 10 minutes, then finely mince it. Set aside.

5. In a larger mortar, mash the garlic with a pestle. Add the shrimp, a few at a time, and mash to a paste. You may have to spoon the paste out of the mortar several times, until the whole batch of shrimp has been mashed.

6. Pound the sugar into the mashed shrimp, then stir in the egg whites. Pound until well blended, adding the pork fat, rice powder, and black pepper.

7. Pour a little peanut oil into a cup and dip the ends of your fingers into it. Take one-twelfth of the shrimp paste (about 2 tablespoonsful) and shape it into an oval around the end of a sugarcane stick, leaving enough stick to use as a handle. Prepare all the sticks, then grill over hot coals or broil in the oven, turning once.

Servings? I like to allow at least four sticks for each person, served up with rice and steamed vegetables or salad. But the Vietnamese stretch it a little farther—and serve it differently. In short, they remove the cooked shrimp paste from the stick, halve it, and use it as a stuffing in rice paper, along with raw vegetables. The raw vegetables often include diced cucumber and mint leaves. Suit yourself. In any case, be sure to save the sugarcane strips. These are chewed for their sweet juice.

GREEK SHRIMP KABOBS

Here's a rather Spartan recipe to try the next time you cook out on the beach.

beheaded or heads-on raw shrimp, large	**sea salt, finely ground**
olive oil	**lemon quarters**

Rig for grilling over charcoal or driftwood. Shuck and skewer the shrimp (deveining if you must), saving the heads, tails, and peelings for stock (page 181) if desired for another recipe. When the coals are hot, brush the shrimp kabobs on both sides with olive oil and sprinkle lightly with fine sea salt. Grill about 4 inches from the hot coals for 2 minutes. Turn and grill for another 2 minutes or so, depending on the size of the shrimp.

Do not overcook. Serve on a bed of rice, with lemon wedges on the side for those who want to squeeze a little juice on the kabobs. Add some grilled eggplant—also brushed with olive oil and sprinkled with salt—and lots of green salad and Greek bread. In the Ionian islands the country people are fond of wild greens either cooked or made into a salad. So try a little young dandelion or chickweed mixed in with the lettuce or spinach. I allow ¾ pound of shrimp per person.

CAMEROON KABOBS WITH UGANDAN GROUNDNUT SAUCE

According to Dave Dewitt's and Chuck Evans's *Hot Sauce Bible,* on which this recipe is based, Cameroon got its name from the Portuguese *camarão,* which means "prawns." The dish is served with a sauce made of peanuts, a rather popular sauce ingredient in Central African and Indonesian cookery.

THE KABOBS

1½ pounds beheaded raw
   shrimp, large or jumbo
   (2 pounds heads-on shrimp)
¼ cup peanut oil
2 tablespoons red pepper
   flakes or ground hot peppers

2 large cloves garlic,
   minced
juice of 1 lemon
1 tablespoon water

THE SAUCE

1 cup peanut butter,
   chunky or smooth
½ pound dried fish
4 medium tomatoes, chopped
2 medium onions, chopped

2 teaspoons peanut oil
2 teaspoons cayenne pepper
1 teaspoon curry powder
salt to taste
2½ cups water

First, prepare the sauce. Soak the fish overnight in water. If convenient, change the water several times. Drain the fish, then
bone and chop it. Heat the oil in a skillet. Sauté the onions for
5 minutes. Add the tomatoes and cook, uncovered, for another
5 minutes. Add the water, fish, peanut butter, cayenne, curry,
and salt if needed. (If you're using highly salted dried fish, additional salt may not be necessary.) Simmer uncovered over very
low heat for 45 minutes, or until the sauce thickens to suit you.
Keep warm.

Shuck the shrimp, deveining if you must. Save the
heads, tails, and peelings for stock (page 181), if needed for
another recipe. Mix the oil, lemon juice, garlic, water, red
pepper flakes, and shrimp in a bowl. Marinate in the refrigerator for 2 hours. Rig for grilling over charcoal. Skewer the
shrimp and heat the marinade until it boils. Grill the kabobs
about 4 inches over the coals for about 2 minutes on each
side, basting a time or two with the boiled marinade. Serve
hot with the Ugandan Groundnut Sauce, or other suitable
African peanut sauce, along with rice and grilled pineapple.
Feeds 2 or more.

GOOD OL' BOY KABOBS

Many backyard chefs are fond of wrapping shrimp in a strip of
bacon and grilling it over charcoal or gas heat. Usually the
shrimp are wrapped individually and pinned with round
toothpicks or small skewers. Of course, they're first dusted
lightly with lemon-pepper or some such seasoning salt,
wrapped with bacon, and grilled until the bacon is ready to
eat, as detailed in the recipe on page 34. For kabobs, the
shrimp can be strung up on the skewer and covered with
bacon in a spiral wrap or perhaps with some ribbon covering

using two strips of bacon. These will drips lots of grease and have to be moved about on the grill to prevent serious flare-ups. Have an extra beer at hand so you won't have to leave the grill for a trip to the refrigerator.

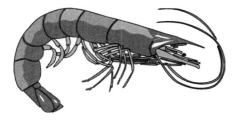

10

Shrimp in Soups and Stews

S hrimp make a happy addition to many seafood soups and stews and medleys, such as the great cioppino, a California creation with fish and shellfish of several sorts—or in bouillabaisse, the great French seafood stew. In some of these the shrimp are optional, if replaced by crab claws or some such shellfish.

In many parts of the country, shrimp is a very important ingredient in gumbo or in soups billed as gumbo. A few soup or stew recipes that lean heavily toward shrimp are included below. Closely related dishes such as Spanish paella and Cajun or Creole jambalaya, both cooked with rice, are covered in chapter 11.

Generally, shrimp used in soups and stews should be beheaded, tailed, and shucked before you add them to the other ingredients. (Deveining is optional.) To cook them whole in the soup or stew makes them more difficult to peel because of the long cooking period. If the peeling is to be done at the table, it's best to add the shrimp only during the last few minutes of cooking, as a rule.

APALACHICOLA GUMBO

All true gumbo should have okra in it, as this one does. A filé gumbo, popular in Louisiana, should be called a filé gumbo. Both okra pods and filé (a powder made from dried sassafras leaves) produce a mucilaginous texture that is essential to gumbo; without it, the dish is simply a soup or stew of some sort. It's best, almost always, to serve the gumbo in a soup bowl with rice. The gumbo goes in first, and a round dollop of rice is added to the center.

**1½ pounds beheaded raw shrimp,
    medium (2 pounds heads-on
    medium shrimp)**
1 pound fresh young okra
2 cups chopped tomatoes
2 stalks celery, chopped
1 large onion, minced
3 cloves garlic, minced
1 cup butter
¼ cup flour

**chopped fresh parsley
    or celery tops**
2 bay leaves
**salt and freshly ground
    black pepper**
Tabasco sauce to taste
**long-grain white rice,
    cooked separately**
water

1. Dress the shrimp, putting the heads (if available), tails, and peelings into a pot (reserve the meats). Cover with 1 quart of water. Add the bay leaves and chopped celery stalks. Bring to a boil, cover, reduce the heat, and simmer for 30 minutes or so. Strain out and discard the solids. Measure 3 cups of stock and set aside. (Add water if you have less than 3 cups of stock.)

2. Melt the butter in a cast-iron stovetop Dutch oven. Sauté the onion and garlic for 5 minutes, stirring with a wooden spoon

as you go. Stir in the flour a little at a time. Cook over very low heat for at least 10 minutes, stirring constantly. Add the tomatoes, parsley, salt, black pepper, and Tabasco. Simmer—but do not boil—for 30 minutes or so.

3. Slice the okra into ½-inch rounds, add them to the pot, and simmer for 20 minutes.

4. Add the shrimp and simmer for about 10 minutes, or until the shrimp are nicely pink. Serve in soup bowls with rice. Feeds 4.

HEADS-UP SHRIMP BISQUE

There are easier recipes for shrimp bisque, but this one fills the bill for something special for culinary sports who don't mind sucking the heads at the table.

3 pounds heads-on shrimp, large (no substitute)
1 cup chopped tomatoes
5 tablespoons flour
⅓ cup cracker crumbs, divided
¼ cup butter
¼ cup bacon drippings or vegetable shortening
¼ cup chopped fresh parsley
¼ cup chopped onion
¼ cup sherry
2 chicken eggs, beaten with a little water
1 tablespoon chopped green bell pepper
1 tablespoon chopped red bell pepper
1 clove garlic, minced
2 bay leaves
½ tablespoon chopped fresh thyme
juice of ½ lemon
1 teaspoon onion juice
½ teaspoon cayenne pepper
½ teaspoon white pepper
salt and black pepper to taste
water

1. Peel and devein the shrimp, saving the heads, peelings, and tails. Scoop out the fat and stuff from the heads, putting it into a pot with 2 quarts of water. Add the shrimp shells, setting the cleaned heads aside. Add the bay leaves and a little salt. Boil for a few minutes. Turn off the heat and let sit.

2. In a skillet, heat the bacon fat. Stir in the flour with a wooden spoon. Cook and stir, cook and stir, until you have a dark roux. Add the onions, bell peppers, and garlic, stirring for about 5 minutes. Add the chopped tomatoes.

3. Strain the stock and put it back onto the pot. Add the roux mixture and half the dressed shrimp. Stir in the thyme, parsley, cayenne, white pepper, and a little salt. Cover and simmer over very low heat for 1 hour.

4. Preheat the oven to 400 degrees. Chop the rest of the shrimp finely, or grind in a food mill. Add about three-quarters of the cracker crumbs along with the beaten eggs, onion juice, salt, and black pepper to taste. Fry this mixture in butter for 5 minutes, stirring as you go. Stuff the mixture into the reserved shrimp heads. (Put any leftover stuffing into the soup pot.) Place the heads into a pan and sprinkle with the remaining cracker crumbs. Bake in the center of the hot oven until browned.

5. Put the heads into the soup, along with the lemon juice and sherry. Simmer for 5 minutes. Serve hot with crusty bread.

Servings? If used as an opening to a larger meal, these measures will serve 6 or 8 people. I can eat a bowl or two for a light lunch, along with plenty of crusty French bread or perhaps saltine crackers.

EASY BISQUE

Here's a relatively easy recipe for bisque. In it I specify 1 pound of peeled and deveined cooked shrimp, which can be leftovers from a shrimp boil or other shrimp feed. Precooked supermarket shrimp also work. If you want to start from scratch, as well you should, boil or steam 1½ pounds of beheaded but unpeeled shrimp or 2 pounds of heads-on shrimp; boil these for 2 or 3 minutes, until they turn pink and can be peeled easily. The recipe works best with medium or small shrimp.

1 pound beheaded, peeled,
   and tailed shrimp, precooked
1 quart milk (divided)
½ cup butter
½ cup sherry
¼ cup finely chopped
   green onion
¼ cup finely chopped celery
   with green tops
¼ cup finely chopped
   red bell pepper

1 tablespoon cornstarch
1 teaspoon Worcestershire
   sauce
½ teaspoon cayenne pepper
½ teaspoon Hungarian
   paprika
salt
chopped fresh parsley
   (for garnish; optional)

Save out about ¼ pound of the shrimp. Put the rest into a blender or food processor, adding 1 cup of the milk along with the cornstarch, Worcestershire, salt, cayenne, and paprika. Blend until the shrimp are finely chopped. In a soup pot or stovetop Dutch oven, sauté the onions, celery, and red bell pepper in the butter for 4 or 5 minutes, stirring as you go with a wooden spoon. Add the contents of the blender and the rest of the milk. Heat until smoking hot. Add the rest of the shrimp. Bring to a simmer—but do not boil. Stir in the sherry and serve immediately in bowls, garnished with a sprinkling of chopped parsley, if you wish. This recipe will serve 6 to 8 people for a soup course.

Note: I sometimes cook this with about a pound of leftover fish in the blender instead of the chopped shrimp. Then I add ¼ pound of small whole shrimp toward the end. For best results, the fish should be mild, white, and lean, such as flounder or largemouth bass.

SHRIMP STEW WITH CORNMEAL DUMPLINGS

Here's a filling dish that I like for lunch on a cold day. It's made with stone-ground cornmeal and won't work with the yellow gritty stuff sold in supermarkets. If you can't obtain this cornmeal readily, scratch the cornmeal dumplings and substitute your grandmother's recipe for wheat-flour dumplings.

THE STEW
2¼ pounds beheaded raw
   shrimp, medium (3 pounds
   heads-on shrimp)
10 small new potatoes
  (golf ball sized)
1 large onion, chopped
1 rib celery with green tops

¼ cup chopped fresh parsley
2 tablespoons chopped fresh
   basil (optional)
1 pod hot red pepper
salt and freshly ground
   black pepper
water to cover

THE DUMPLINGS
1½ cups white stone-ground cornmeal
1 to 1¼ cups hot broth from the shrimp pot
1 teaspoon salt

1. Wash the shrimp and place them, whole, into a pot of rapidly boiling water. There should be enough water to cover the shrimp by at least 2 inches. Bring to a new boil and cook for

2 minutes. Scoop the shrimp out of the pot with a hand strainer and drain in a colander. Start peeling the shrimp as soon as they are cool enough. Put the peelings (heads, shells, and tails) back into the pot of water, saving the meats in a bowl. When all the shrimp have been peeled, put the chopped celery and red pepper into the pot. Boil for about 20 minutes. (During this time you can devein the shrimp, if you're feeding squeamish guests.)

2. Strain the broth into a large bowl. Discard the solids. Pour the stock back into the pot and bring to a boil. Add the potatoes, onion, parsley, and basil, if used. Bring to a new boil, reduce the heat, cover, and simmer until the potatoes are done, about 20 minutes or so, depending on their size.

3. While you're waiting, mix the cornmeal and salt in a bowl. Add just enough of the hot shrimp stock to make a dough— about 1 cup. Shape the dough into small bite-sized oblong rounds. Set aside.

4. When the potatoes are done, add the cooked shrimp to the pot. There should be plenty of stock left, bringing the liquid level to the top of the other contents; if not, add a little hot water. Bring to a boil, adding salt and freshly ground black pepper to taste. Drop the dumplings gently into the stew, working around the edge of the pot. Simmer (do not boil) for 15 minutes. Gently stir the stew a time or two, but do not break up the dumplings; at the same time, you want to dislodge just enough of the cornmeal to thicken the stew. (If this doesn't work, mash one of the dumplings into a little hot broth, then stir the paste into the stew.) Serve hot in large soup bowls, along with saltine crackers or crusty bread, topping individual bowls with freshly ground black pepper, if desired. These measures feed 6 or more, as the dumplings are quite filling. If I am eating alone on a cold day, however, I can finish off the pot in three sittings.

SHRIMP ÉTOUFFÉE

This old Cajun dish is usually cooked with crawfish in the bayou country of southwestern Louisiana, but shrimp as well as crabmeat and lobster also work, if adjustments are made. It's best to start with whole heads-on shrimp, making a good stock. (If your shrimp are already beheaded and peeled, alas, use about 1½ cups of them, along with some chicken or fish stock.) After boiling, the shrimp can be deveined, but I don't think any self-respecting Cajun will waste time doing this, unless perhaps he is courting. The roux, however, is a more serious matter and requires much stirring.

2 pounds heads-on shrimp, medium
⅓ cup bacon drippings or lard
¼ cup all-purpose flour
1 cup chopped onions
½ cup chopped celery with some green tops
⅓ cup chopped red bell pepper
⅓ cup chopped green bell pepper
⅓ cup green onion tops or fresh chives
3 cloves garlic, minced
1 tablespoon minced fresh parsley or cilantro
juice of ½ lemon
½ teaspoon red pepper flakes
salt and freshly ground black pepper
rice (cooked separately)
water

1. Bring half a pot of water to boil over high heat and add the shrimp. Bring to a new boil for 2 minutes, or until the shrimp turn nicely pink. Remove the shrimp with a slotted spoon, placing them in a colander close to the pot. When the shrimp have cooled down enough to handle, behead, shuck, and tail them, placing the meat in a bowl and putting all the trimmings back into the pot. Keep the peeled shrimp warm. Boil the shrimp trimmings until the stock reduces by about half. Strain and set aside.

2. In a stovetop Dutch oven or similar pot, heat the bacon drip-pings, stirring in the flour. Cook over low heat for at least 20 minutes, stirring as you go with a wooden spoon, until you have a nice brown roux. Add the onions, garlic, red bell pep-per, green bell pepper, celery, green onion tops, and parsley. Cover and cook over low heat for 20 minutes; stir often—if you don't, the bottom may burn. Mix in the peeled shrimp, lemon juice, red pepper flakes, salt, and black pepper. Add about 2 cups of the hot shrimp stock and bring to a boil. (If you don't have 2 cups of stock, fill in with hot water.) Quickly add the dressed shrimp. Heat through for 2 or 3 minutes, adding more salt or pepper if needed. Stir in more hot stock if needed to make enough gravy to wet down the rice.

3. Serve in deep plates or large bowls over a bed of rice, along with crusty New Orleans bread and good red wine. Feeds 4, if you've got enough rice and bread.

EASY SHRIMP SOUP

I often put a few shrimp into soups and stews without having a recipe to follow. Usually, the shrimp should be peeled. If I start out with fresh shrimp, I either boil them for 2 or 3 minutes or sauté them in a little butter before proceeding. Starting with a condensed cream soup from the supermarket makes this process very easy. The ingredients list below calls for cream of mushroom, but others, such as cream of celery, also work.

1 can cream of mushroom soup	fresh mushrooms (optional)
	butter (optional)
precooked shrimp, peeled	water

Sauté the mushrooms in a little butter for about 5 minutes. Add the shrimp. In a soup pot, heat the cream of mushroom soup with 1 can of water. Add the mushrooms and shrimp and simmer (do not boil) for a few minutes. Serve hot, along with freshly ground black pepper. Feeds 2.

Variations: Sauté some chopped onion along with the mushrooms. You can also use cream of celery soup and lots of fresh mushrooms. A little wine won't hurt a thing. Experiment. Note that using whole shrimp, or perhaps shrimp halves, gives you a chunky soup. If you want something smoother, try grinding the shrimp in a food mill or processor.

AZTEC SHRIMP SOUP

The Aztecs of Mexico made this soup with fresh shrimp, brought into Mexico City from the Gulf of Mexico or from the Pacific by runners. The recipe also calls for toasted dried shrimp, an important ingredient before the days of mechanical refrigeration. I first ran across the recipe in *Cuisine of the Water Gods,* an excellent Mexican seafood book by Patricia Quintana, but I changed the recipe considerably. The original called for fresh *masa,* which may be hard to find. I have changed it to an equal amount of pureed canned hominy, which is available in supermarkets. Essentially, however, it is an Aztec recipe.

2¼ pounds beheaded raw
   shrimp, medium (3 pounds
   heads-on shrimp)
½ cup dried shrimp
1 cup canned hominy
3 quarts hot Shrimp Stock
   (page 181) or fish stock
1 quart hot water
⅓ cup lard or olive oil
½ pound tomatillos, husked

1 medium onion, diced
12 dried ancho, chilacate,
   guajillo, or cascabel chili
   peppers
4 dried de arbol, red Tabasco,
   or other small chili peppers
4 cloves garlic, peeled
salt to taste
1½ teaspoons cumin seeds
lime halves (for garnish)

1. Heat a cast-iron skillet and toast the dried shrimp. Then grind the dried shrimp in a food mill, or with a mortar and pestle. Set aside.

2. Carefully seed and devein the peppers, preferably with the aid of rubber gloves. Toast the peppers in the skillet over high heat, stirring with a wooden spoon and, in the same motion, pressing down with the back of the spoon. Rinse the toasted peppers, cover with the hot water, and soak for 1 hour. Drain the peppers and puree them with a little of the water and the onion and tomatillos, adding the garlic, cumin, and salt until you have a smooth paste. Put the paste into a stovetop Dutch oven or other suitable pot. Cook over medium heat until the sauce thickens.

3. Place the hominy into a bowl and moisten it with a little of the stock. Puree until you have a doughlike paste, rather thin. Add this to the chili paste and cook for 10 minutes. Add the rest of the stock and cook, uncovered, until you have a soupy texture.

4. Add the raw shrimp and the toasted dried shrimp. Cook for 20 minutes. Serve in deep soup bowls, with lime halves and plenty of fresh corn tortillas on the side. Remember that this is a messy dish to eat, since the shrimp have to be peeled at the table. Have plenty of napkins or towels. Feeds 6 to 8.

11

Shrimp with Pasta and Rice

Shrimp goes well with whole-grain products such as pasta, and it's especially welcome in rice dishes. Here are my favorites.

SHRIMP JAMBALAYA

By definition, a jambalaya must have both ham and rice. The shrimp, oysters, and sausage used in this recipe make the dish even better. It's best to cook this recipe in a large 13-inch jambalaya skillet, but a stovetop Dutch oven will do.

1½ pounds beheaded raw
   shrimp, medium (2 pounds
   heads-on shrimp)
1 pound smoked andouille
   link sausage, cut into wheels

½ cup chopped red bell pepper
½ cup chopped green
   bell pepper
¼ cup chopped green
   onion tops

1 cup diced fresh lean pork
(½-inch cubes)
1 cup diced baked cured ham
(½-inch cubes)
1 pint freshly shucked oysters
with liquor
4 cups chopped onions
4 cloves garlic, minced
1½ cups long-grain rice
¼ cup butter
2 stalks celery with tops,
chopped

¼ cup chopped fresh parsley
1 tablespoon salt
½ teaspoon freshly ground
black pepper
½ teaspoon cayenne pepper
½ teaspoon dried thyme
½ teaspoon crushed bay leaves
oyster liquor as needed
salted water

1. Boil the shrimp in salted water for 2 or 3 minutes, until they turn nicely pink and shuck easily. Strain out the shrimp and shuck them, putting the heads, tails, and peelings back into the pot along with the celery. Simmer for 20 or 30 minutes, then strain through a sieve, throwing out the solids. Save 3 cups. If you don't have that much liquid, add a little oyster liquor or water.

2. Melt the butter in a large skillet, then sauté the ham, sausage, and pork for 10 minutes, stirring from time to time with a wooden spoon. Add the onions, peppers, garlic, and parsley, along with the black pepper, cayenne pepper, thyme, bay leaves, and salt. Cook for 30 minutes, stirring often. Add the rice. Cook for 5 minutes.

3. Add the shrimp stock. Increase the heat, bringing the liquid to a boil. Add the oysters. Cover and simmer—but do not boil—for 1 hour over very low heat, stirring gently from time to time. Add a little oyster liquid (or water, if necessary) as needed to keep the dish from drying out. Remove the cover and simmer until the rice dries out a little, like a pilaf, stirring gently with a wooden spoon.

4. Serve hot in deep plates or wide soup bowls, along with plenty of crusty French bread. Feeds 4 to 6.

TAMPA BAY POLENTA

This unusual shrimp dish is from the old Cuban community in Tampa, Florida, where Cubans were employed in the cigar industry and where shrimp still swim free for the taking. I use fresh red cayenne peppers in this dish, but any hot chili can be used, either fresh, dried, or canned. Remember that most of the heat in a pepper is in its seeds and inner pith, so remove these unless you want a fiery dish.

1½ pounds beheaded raw shrimp, medium (2 pounds heads-on raw shrimp)	2 tablespoons tomato paste
	2 tablespoons olive oil
	1 or 2 chopped fresh red Tabasco peppers, to taste
1 cup yellow stone-ground cornmeal	1 tablespoon freshly ground cumin
1 cup chopped onion	salt
2 cloves garlic, minced	water

Boil the shrimp in salted water for 2 or 3 minutes. Drain and peel the shrimp, throwing the heads, tails, and peelings back into the pot. Boil for 20 minutes or so, then strain out the stock and discard the solids.

Pour the stock and enough water to make up a quart of liquid into a heavy saucepan or a stovetop Dutch oven. Add the cornmeal and a little salt. Bring to a boil, then reduce the heat to very low. Quickly heat the olive oil in a saucepan and sauté the onion, peppers, and garlic for 4 or 5 minutes, or until the onion starts to turn brown around the edges. To the saucepan add the shrimp and tomato paste. Cook for 3 minutes, stirring as you go with a wooden spoon. Add the shrimp mixture to the cornmeal mixture, stirring it in with the wooden spoon. Also stir in the cumin and a little more salt. Cook for 35 minutes over low heat, stirring frequently, or until the mixture is very thick. Serve hot or refrigerate and serve cold.

Variation: I like to sprinkle a little grated Parmesan cheese over the dish during the last few minutes of cooking. A few strips of roasted red bell pepper arranged on top also make the dish look as good as it tastes.

LINGUINE WITH SHRIMP

I stand in debt to my sister-in-law, Mary Catherine Livingston, for this recipe, and to my brother, Col. Ira L. Livingston, Ret., for his enthusiasm about it, which overcame my apathy for yet another pasta creation. This is good stuff, made, they say, with frozen shrimp.

2 pounds unpeeled, beheaded raw shrimp, medium	2 tablespoons chopped fresh parsley
1 pound dry linguine	2 teaspoons olive oil
2 ounces day-old Italian bread, coarsely crumbled	more olive oil
2 tablespoons freshly grated Parmesan cheese	2 cloves garlic, minced
more Parmesan to taste	¼ teaspoon red pepper flakes
1 small can anchovy fillets with oil (½-ounce size)	salted water

Shuck the shrimp, pull off the tail fins, devein (if you must), and set aside. In lightly salted water, cook the linguine al dente. Drain and toss the linguine with 2 tablespoons of grated

Parmesan and 2 teaspoons of olive oil. Keep warm. In a skillet, cook the anchovies and the oil from the can, stirring as you go, until the fillets have broken up. Add the bread crumbs, garlic, and red pepper flakes. Cook until the crumbs are brown, stirring as you go. Put a little more olive oil into the skillet and stir-fry the shrimp until they're nicely pink, about 3 minutes. Add to the pasta mixture. Sprinkle with parsley. Serve immediately, along with more Parmesan for sprinkling on each serving to taste. Serve with a big tossed salad (with plenty of fresh tomatoes) dressed with oil and vinegar, crusty Italian bread, and red vino. Feeds 4 or more.

CROSS CREEK PURLOO

The crackers of rural Florida make good use of rice dishes containing a little meat. These are usually served as a side dish to a meal, or at an outdoor church dinner or perhaps a family reunion. Purloo—as pilaf is called thereabouts—also makes a good lunch and can save the evening meal, in case the meat supplies are low.

1½ pounds beheaded raw shrimp, medium (2 pounds heads-on shrimp)	1 cup uncooked long-grain rice
	1 medium onion, chopped
2 slices salt pork (bacon slice sized)	salt and red pepper flakes to taste
	4 cups water

Dress the shrimp, saving the heads, shells, and tails for stock (page 181) if wanted for another recipe. Fry the salt pork in a cast-iron skillet until crisp, then, using a wooden spoon, turn it out, grease and all, into a black iron pot. Add the water and bring to a rolling boil. Add the remaining ingredients to the pot, bring to a new boil, reduce the heat to very low, cover, and simmer for 20 minutes. Remove the cover and steam off most of the water, fluffing the purloo a time or two with a wooden spatula to keep it from burning on the bottom. (Unlike some pilaf, this dish can be quite moist—but not downright soupy.) Serve as a side dish to fried barnyard chicken or young squirrel, sliced tomatoes, and boiled okra (if this is for Sunday dinner, use only whole small okra pods, little-finger sized), along with perhaps swamp cabbage (canned as heart of palm). Feeds 2 or more.

PAELLA

A paella pan—about 15 inches wide and shallow with slanted sides—was traditionally used for cooking this recipe. This thing was designed for cooking over an open fire and doesn't work well on a modern stovetop, because the burners don't heat the pan evenly. I recommend using a large electric skillet, suitable for serving. Note that the measures below require a large skillet to contain everything. A stovetop Dutch oven can also be used, if necessary.

The original paella was made with rabbit or chicken, but these days shellfish have become more important in most such recipes. In my book shrimp tops the list.

¾ pound beheaded raw
  shrimp, medium (1 pound
  heads-on shrimp)
½ pound crab claws, cracked
½ pound firm fish fillets, cut
  into 1-inch chunks
2 dozen freshly shucked oysters
1 dozen fresh mussels
½ pound chorizo, cut into
  ½-inch wheels

2 cups chopped fresh tomatoes
1½ cups chopped onions
10 cloves garlic, minced
½ green bell pepper, cut into
  thin strips
½ red bell pepper, cut into
  thin strips
1 cup olive oil
salt and freshly ground
  black pepper

1 fryer chicken, cut into serving pieces	**½ teaspoon Spanish (hot) paprika**
3 cups uncooked Valencia or other short-grain rice	**½ teaspoon ground saffron boiling water**

1. Rig for steaming. Wash, trim, and steam the mussels. (Discard any that do not open.) Set the mussels aside, leaving them in their shells over the hot water.

2. Heat the olive oil in a large skillet over medium-high heat. Brown the chicken, turning from time to time. Add the chorizo slices and cook for another 3 or 4 minutes or so, stirring with a wooden spoon. Place the chicken and chorizo on a brown bag to drain.

3. Sauté the onions in the remaining oil for 5 minutes. Add the tomatoes. Increase the heat to high and cook for about 5 minutes. Add the red pepper, green pepper, garlic, salt, black pepper, and Spanish paprika. Cook for 5 minutes. Add the rice and cook for 5 minutes, stirring constantly, until it starts to turn brown. Add the chicken and sausage pieces, along with 4 cups of boiling water. Mix the saffron into a little more boiling water, then stir it into the pan contents.

4. When the liquid starts to boil nicely, add the crab claws. Stir in 3 more cups of boiling water. Cook for 3 or 4 minutes, then add the shrimp and fish chunks. Cook for another 3 or 4 minutes, then add the oysters. Cook for a few minutes, until the oysters start to curl around the edges. Take the pan off the heat and arrange the steamed mussels on top.

5. Place the pan on trivets in the middle of the table. Spoon the paella directly onto preheated plates. Have at hand plenty of crusty hot bread and good red wine. This recipe feeds 8 to 10 people.

SHRIMP AND WHOLE HOMINY

Here's one of my favorite combinations, a dish that has color appeal as well as taste. For convenience, I usually make it with canned whole-kernel hominy, available at the supermarket, but properly cooked pozole (dried hominy) or freshly made pre-cooked hominy also works.

1½ pounds beheaded raw
   shrimp, large (2 pounds
   heads-on shrimp)
4 to 6 slices smoked bacon
1 can golden hominy
   (16-ounce size)

1 medium to large onion
1 large red bell pepper
1 fresh green jalapeño
salt and freshly ground black
   pepper to taste
water

Boil the shrimp in salted water for 2 or 3 minutes, or until nicely pink. Drain and dress the shrimp, saving the heads, tails, and peelings for stock, if needed for another recipe (page 181). Roast and seed the bell pepper, then cut it into thin strips lengthwise. Also, peel the onion and cut it into thin strips lengthwise. Seed and chop the jalapeño. In a large skillet, fry the bacon until crisp. Remove the bacon, draining it on a brown bag. In the bacon drippings, sauté the onion and jalapeño for 4 or 5 minutes. Add the drained hominy and roasted bell pepper. Cook for several minutes, stirring and tossing a time or two. Mix in the shrimp. Cook for another 4 or 5 minutes. Serve hot, with the bacon on the side, along with, perhaps, vine-ripened tomato slices. Feeds 2 to 4 for lunch.

SHRIMP AND RICE IN THE SKILLET

This recipe is great for using leftover boiled shrimp. It's even better when freshly boiled or steamed shrimp are used. Any good skillet will do, if it's large enough. A large electric skillet suitable for serving (with the aid of a trivet) is perfect.

2 cups chopped precooked shrimp
3 cups steamed long-grain white rice
8 ounces fresh mushrooms, sliced
1 cup green onions with tops,
   chopped

¼ cup olive oil
2 tablespoons soy sauce
2 chicken eggs, whisked
salt and freshly ground
   black pepper

Heat the olive oil for a few minutes in a skillet. Sauté the mushrooms for 5 or 6 minutes. Add the shrimp and cook for a minute or two, stirring constantly with a wooden spoon. Stir in the eggs, salt, and pepper. Add the rice, soy sauce, and green onions. Heat for about 5 minutes, stirring as you go. Serve hot. Feeds 4 to 6.

Note: If you don't have quite enough leftover shrimp to make 2 cups, add some diced cooked ham or leftover turkey.

12

Shrimp in Pies and Casseroles

Anumber of pies and countless casseroles can be made with the aid of shrimp, either as a specified ingredient in someone's recipe or as a substitute for lump crabmeat. Frozen and precooked shrimp—even canned—can be used in most cases, but, almost always, freshly boiled shrimp are better. Here are three of my favorites.

LONG ISLAND PIE

This old recipe (modified considerably) is from Long Island, where eels used to be more popular than in most other parts of the country. I use prepared tomato-based salsa, but a freshly made Creole sauce can also be used. If you like the flavor of fresh eel (which, if properly prepared, is one of the best fish that swims, provided that it's not merely fried), use a mild salsa; if not, go higher on the heat scale or substitute a mild fish of firm flesh. Both the eel and the shrimp should be very fresh. For convenience, a piecrust from the supermarket is acceptable, but good cooks will want to use their favorite recipe. I like to cover this pie with strips of crust, making a lattice.

1 fresh eel, about 2 pounds
1½ pounds beheaded raw shrimp,
   medium (2 pounds heads-on
   shrimp)
½ cup melted butter
1 cup Shrimp Stock (page 181)
   or clam broth

1 cup chunky salsa
juice of 1 lemon
pie pastry, cut into strips
salt and pepper
water

Preheat the oven to 350 degrees. Skin and fillet the eel, then poach it in salted water for 10 minutes. Boil the shrimp for 3 minutes, then behead and peel them; devein if you like. Make a stock with the heads and peelings (page 181). Cut the shrimp meats in half and cut the poached eel fillets into 1-inch segments. Pour about half of the melted butter on the eel and shrimp, tossing lightly. Butter a deep ovenproof dish suitable for serving. Place about half the shrimp on the bottom and layer on about half the eel. Pour the salsa, spreading it evenly. Add another layer of eel and one of shrimp. Mix the lemon juice and broth in with the rest of the butter, adding a little salt and black pepper to taste. Pour the mixture evenly over the pie filling. Cover with strips of pie pastry, making a lattice. Bake in the center of the oven for 35 minutes. Serve hot, along with hot biscuit halves and green peas or other suitable vegetables. Feeds 4 or more.

    Note: Smoked eel is also very good in this recipe. Use about ½ pound instead of the eel fillets.

SHRIMP AND WILD RICE CASSEROLE

More and more American cooks are relying on canned soups as an ingredient in various dishes. Thick creamed soups are especially good in casseroles, and offer an easy way to vary the recipe. If the ingredients list calls for cream of mushroom soup, the creative cook may want to substitute cream of celery, for example, along with a few sliced fresh mushrooms.

¾ pound beheaded raw shrimp, medium or small (1 pound heads-on shrimp; ½ pound fully shucked shrimp)
1 can cream of chicken soup
2 cups precooked wild rice
½ cup cubed sharp cheddar cheese
8 ounces sliced mushrooms
2 tablespoons chopped green onions with part of tops

2 tablespoons chopped red bell pepper
2 tablespoons melted butter
juice of 1 lemon
1 teaspoon lemon zest
1 teaspoon white wine Worcestershire sauce
½ teaspoon dry mustard
½ teaspoon white pepper
salt to taste

Boil the shrimp for 2 or 3 minutes. Behead, shuck, and tail the shrimp, saving the trimmings and boiling liquid for stock (page 181), if needed for another recipe. Preheat the oven to 375 degrees and grease a 1½-quart ovenproof dish suitable for serving. Mix the peeled shrimp and the rest of the ingredients. Bake in the center of the oven for 30 or 35 minutes. Feeds 4 to 6.

CHARLESTON CASSEROLE

This is a very old Low Country dish. I like to serve it for lunch, or as a side dish for an evening meal.

1½ pounds beheaded raw
   shrimp, medium (2 pounds
   heads-on shrimp)
1 cup milk
¾ cup chopped green onions
   with part of tops
½ cup chopped red bell pepper
3 slices good white bread
2 large chicken eggs, whisked
2 tablespoons butter

2 tablespoons chopped
   fresh parsley
1 tablespoon dry sherry
1 teaspoon Worcestershire
   sauce
¼ teaspoon freshly ground
   black pepper
¼ teaspoon cayenne pepper
⅛ teaspoon mace

Preheat the oven to 325 degrees and butter a 2½-quart casserole dish suitable for serving. Remove the crusts from the bread and discard them. Cut the bread into pieces and soak in the milk. Behead, peel, and devein the shrimp. Mix all the ingredients (except the butter) in a bowl. Turn the mixture out into the casserole dish, smooth it out, and dot it with the 2 tablespoons of butter. Place in the center of the preheated oven and bake for 40 to 50 minutes, until the top is nicely browned. Serve hot directly from the baking dish. Feeds 2 to 4.

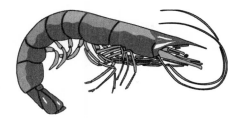

13

Shrimp in the Stuffing

A few shrimp can be used to advantage in many recipes for dressings and stuffings, but the best of these involve such fish dishes as Pompano en Papillote, a recipe created at Antoine's in New Orleans. The pompano fillet is the main ingredient, and the shrimp is merely a part of the stuffing or dressing, along with crabmeat. Another recipe of this type is Fillet of Sole Marguery à la Diamond Jim, named for Diamond Jim Brady, the flamboyant American millionaire, in which sole is "stuffed" with shrimp and oysters. I consider both dishes to be dressed with the shrimp mixture, however, not stuffed. They're good, though. For the Diamond Jim creation I recommend the recipe in the *Heritage Cook Book,* published some time ago by *Better Homes and Gardens.* My take on Pompano en Papillote is covered below, following less Frenchy fare. Also see the Shrimp and Fish Fillet recipe on page 63.

STUFFED RED SNAPPER

Although red snapper is ideal for this recipe, any good baking fish can be used, including one of my favorites—freshwater black bass, largemouth or smallmouth.

1 red snapper, 4- to 5-pound size
1½ pounds beheaded raw
   shrimp, medium (2 pounds
   heads-on shrimp)
1 cup butter
2 cups bread crumbs
1 cup chopped onions
1 cup chopped celery with tops
2 chicken eggs
1 or 2 hot red chili peppers,
   seeded and minced

1 red bell pepper, roasted,
   seeded, and minced
1 tablespoon chopped
   fresh parsley
3 thin slices tomato
3 thin slices onion
olive oil
salt and pepper to taste
water

1. Boil the shrimp in lightly salted water for 2 or 3 minutes, or until they turn pink and peel easily. Shuck the shrimp, putting the heads, tails, and peelings back into the pot. Boil the stock until it's reduced by about half. Strain, discarding the solids. Finely mince or grind half the shrimp meats; set this aside, separate from the others.

2. Heat the butter in a stovetop Dutch oven or suitable pot. Sauté the onions and celery for 5 minutes, stirring as you go with a wooden spoon. Add the chicken eggs, minced shrimp, whole shrimp, parsley, minced red pepper, minced chili pepper, salt, and black pepper. Moisten the bread crumbs well with the reduced stock. Mix the bread crumbs into the contents of the pot, adding a little more stock if needed to make a moist stuffing. (Refrigerate what's left of the stock, if you want it for another recipe.)

3. Preheat the oven to 350 degrees. Scale and gut the fish, leaving the head intact. Tear off a large sheet of heavy aluminum foil. Center the fish on the foil. Stuff the cavity with the stuffing mixture. Place any remaining stuffing around the fish. Alternate the tomato and onion slices on the fish and drizzle with a little olive oil. Fold the foil over the fish, then seal the edges with tight double folds. Place the foil into a shallow baking pan.

4. Bake in the center of the oven for 40 minutes. Open the foil and bake until the fish and stuffing are lightly browned. Carefully place the fish, whole, onto a heated serving platter and send to the table. Have ready plenty of white rice, salad or vegetables, and crusty bread. I'll want some red wine with my serving, but white will do. Feeds 4 to 6.

FLOUNDER STUFFED WITH SHRIMP

Stuffed flatfish makes a very attractive and tasty dish, especially when stuffed with shrimp or crabmeat, or perhaps a combination of both. I highly recommend this dish for summer flounder, sand dabs, and other small flatfish of ¾ to 1 pound each. In other words, serve a whole stuffed fish for each plate. The recipe has been adapted here from my *Saltwater Fish Cookbook*. The measures listed below feed 6 people, but can be adjusted easily. It's best to make the stuffing first, preferably with freshly boiled shrimp. Precooked market shrimp or canned shrimp can also be used.

THE SHRIMP STUFFING

1 pound boiled and peeled shrimp, medium*

2 cups soft bread cubes

2 chicken eggs, whisked

½ rib celery with green tops, finely chopped

¼ green bell pepper, finely chopped

⅓ cup butter

1 medium onion, finely chopped

3 cloves garlic, finely chopped

¼ red bell pepper, finely chopped

1 tablespoon finely chopped fresh parsley

salt and pepper to taste

In a skillet over medium heat, sauté the onion, garlic, bell peppers, celery, and parsley in the butter for 3 or 4 minutes. Stir in the shrimp, bread cubes, chicken eggs, salt, and pepper; turn off the heat but leave the skillet on the burner while you prepare the flounder and preheat the oven to 350 degrees.

*If you boil fresh shrimp for this recipe, start with 1½ pounds of beheaded raw shrimp or 2 pounds of heads-on shrimp.

THE FISH

6 fresh small flounder, ¾ to 1 pound each

¾ cup butter

juice of 3 lemons

2 teaspoons salt

Hungarian paprika

When you dress the fish, leave the heads on unless you think your guests might object. (Remember that flatfish will have both eyes looking up.) Lay the fish on its flattest side, eyes up; then, with the small, sharp blade of a pocketknife, make a cut dead center from head to tail. Next, carefully work the knife blade along the backbone and rib bones on either side of the cut. This will form a nice pocket for the stuffing. Note that the stuffing will be exposed on top, from one end of the fish to the other, making a very attractive and easy-to-eat dish.

Stuff each fish liberally. Quickly melt the butter, mixing in the lemon juice and salt. Brush the stuffed fish with the butter mix. Place each fish on a large sheet of lightly greased heavy-duty aluminum foil. Fold the foil up and over the fish, bringing the ends together. Make a 1-inch fold along the edge of the foil, then make another fold in the first fold. The idea is to seal in the

steam to help cook the fish. Place the packages on a large baking sheet (or on two baking sheets if needed) and cook them in
the preheated oven for 20 minutes. Then switch the oven heat to
broil, open the packages, baste again with the lemon-butter mix,
sprinkle the stuffing with paprika, and broil until the stuffing
starts to brown. Serve hot.

Note: You can also cook this dish on a grill or in the coals of a
fire. Merely put the sealed package on the grill over a hot fire for 25
minutes, or put the package directly onto hot coals for 20 minutes.

POMPANO EN PAPILLOTE

Traditionally, a whole fish of about 1 pound is served to each person, and each fish is cooked separately. That is, each fish has its
own bag. It's really best to leave the heads on the fish, unless
you're feeding squeamish eaters. Also, if you've got larger pompano you can cook this dish with ½-pound fillets, allowing one
for each plate. Don't whisper my words in the French Quarter of
New Orleans, but some of the other small jacks, such as the look
down, are just as good as pompano in this recipe, if freshly
caught, promptly drawn, and quickly iced. In any case, the measures below, designed for two plates, can be increased as needed.

2 pompano fillets (or other
  good fillets), about ½ pound
  each
1 cup chopped shrimp
1 cup crabmeat
1 cup fish stock or Shrimp
  Stock (page 181)
1 large onion, chopped
2 green onions with tops,
  chopped

4 ounces fresh mushrooms,
  sliced
2 thin slices lemon
½ cup white wine
½ cup butter
2 chicken egg yolks
1 tablespoon all-purpose
  flour
salt and pepper to taste

Preheat the oven to 400 degrees. Cut two pieces of parchment paper into heart shapes, each large enough to completely enclose a fillet. Make a paste with the flour and a little of the stock; set aside. Melt the butter in a skillet. Sauté the fillets for a few minutes, turning once. Carefully place each on a heated plate. Sauté the shrimp, crabmeat, onion, green onion, and mushrooms for 4 or 5 minutes, stirring with a wooden spoon from time to time. Add the remaining stock to the skillet, then stir in the flour paste, egg yolks, salt, and pepper. Place a fillet skin-side down onto one side of a parchment heart. Spoon over each fillet about half of the sauce from the skillet. Top with a lemon slice. Fold the parchment over and seal by folding the edges up and in. Prepare the other fillet. Place both packages on a cookie sheet and bake in the center of the oven for 25 minutes. Place the packages on individual plates and cut large Xs into the top. Open up the parchment and serve hot. Feeds 2.

14

Shrimp in Appetizers, Sandwiches, and Salads

old boiled shrimp—even leftovers—are great for appetizers and salads, and recipes abound for such favorites as shrimp cocktails. Even shrimp sandwiches offer some pleasant surprises, and American culinary sports who enjoy shrimp seviche south of the border may be inspired to hazard a live shrimp in the Japanese tradition.

Finger Foods and Dips

Shrimp cooked with the tails attached make ideal finger food simply because they have a built-in handle. If served peeled and without the tail, they should be accompanied by small forks, skewers, or round toothpicks. Many of the recipes throughout this book can be used as finger food, either as appetizers or as a main meal. Try fried or boiled shrimp served in a conically rolled newspaper, similar to the British fish-and-chips.

In addition to the recipes below, see the sauces listed in chapter 16, many of which can be used with finger food.

SHRIMP DIP

The shrimp and other ingredients used in this recipe can be finely chopped with a chef's knife or prepared in a food mill of some sort. I make the dip with a handheld cranked rotary chopper, in which case the ingredients are loaded into the machine in chunks and taken out as a dip. The dip should be made a day ahead of its intended use, but you can get by with refrigerating it for several hours, if necessary.

1½ pounds beheaded raw
   shrimp, small (2 pounds
   heads-on shrimp)
8 ounces cream cheese
1 cup mayonnaise
1 small rib celery with green
   tops, chopped
1 medium to large onion,
   chopped

2 cloves garlic, minced
½ cup chopped green onion
   tops or fresh chives
¼ cup fresh lemon juice
1 tablespoon Worcestershire
   sauce
Tabasco sauce to taste
salt to taste
Hungarian paprika (optional)

Set the cream cheese out of the refrigerator so that it will reach room temperature. Boil the shrimp in salted water for 3 or 4 minutes, or until they turn nicely pink. Cool and peel. (Be sure to save the heads, peelings, and tail fins for Shrimp Stock, page 181.) If you're using a chef's knife, finely chop or mince the shrimp and vegetables. Mix all the minced ingredients in a bowl. Add the cream cheese, mayonnaise, Tabasco, Worcestershire, and lemon juice, along with salt to taste. Put the mixture into a serving dish. Refrigerate for 24 hours, giving the flavors a chance to mingle. Sprinkle the dip lightly with Hungarian paprika, if you want a little color, and serve with crackers.

POTTED SHRIMP

I sometimes make potted shrimp from leftovers, but, of course, freshly boiled or steamed shrimp can be used to advantage.

1 pound fully shucked boiled
   shrimp, minced*
¼ cup butter, softened

2 tablespoons fresh lemon juice
⅛ teaspoon mace
salt and white pepper to taste

Put all the ingredients into an electric blender. Blend for 8 to 10 seconds, until smooth. Using a rubber scraper, pack the mix into a small bowl or mold. Refrigerate. When you're ready to serve, demold the shrimp onto a small serving plate or platter. I serve this with a small knife and crackers.

*If you're starting from scratch, use 1½ pounds of beheaded raw shrimp or 2
   pounds of heads-on shrimp. Boil for 3 minutes, cool, and peel.

EASY SHRIMP COCKTAIL

Here's an easy recipe for shrimp cocktail, served in a cocktail glass and eaten with a small fork or even round toothpicks. Small precooked cocktail shrimp can be purchased, but it's really better to cook your own. Increase the measures as needed.

1½ pounds beheaded raw
   shrimp, small (2 pounds
   heads-on raw shrimp)
1 cup prepared chili
   sauce

½ cup mayonnaise
1 tablespoon freshly grated
   horseradish
sprigs of fresh parsley
   (for garnish)

Boil the shrimp for about 2 minutes (if they're quite small). Dress the shrimp, saving the heads, tails, and peelings for stock if desired (see page 181). Chill the peeled shrimp. Mix the chili sauce, mayonnaise, and horseradish. Put the shrimp into cocktail glasses, cover with the sauce, and garnish with a sprig or two of fresh parsley. Serves 4 to 6.

Note: If you have larger shrimp, cook them a bit longer. Behead and peel them, leaving the tails intact. Arrange the shrimp around the edge of a shallow cocktail glass, leaving the tails sticking out. Pour the cocktail sauce in the middle and eat with the fingers, permitting your guests to dip each shrimp in the sauce.

PICKLED SHRIMP

The pickling spice mix used in this recipe can be purchased at the supermarket. If it's not to be found in the spice racks, try the canning section. I use large widemouthed Mason jars for pickling.

GROUP I

3 pounds beheaded raw shrimp, medium to large (4 pounds heads-on shrimp)
1 cup chopped celery with tops
¼ cup pickling spice

4 bay leaves
1 tablespoon salt
sliced onions
water

GROUP II

1 cup olive oil
1 cup white vinegar
1 large red bell pepper, seeded and finely diced

1 tablespoon celery seeds
1 tablespoon salt
½ tablespoon red pepper flakes

Put a gallon of water into a pot and bring it to a boil, adding the salt, celery, pickling spice, and bay leaves. Add the shrimp. Bring to a new boil. Cook until the shrimp turn pink—about 3 minutes. Cool, peel, and devein the shrimp. (To make stock, if wanted, save the head and peelings. Proceed with the recipe on page 181.) Place a layer of sliced onions in the bottom of a jar (two 1-quart Mason jars will do for this recipe, or you can use a larger container with a tight lid). Add a layer of shrimp, another layer of onions, and so on, ending with onions. Put all the group II ingredients into a pot and bring to a quick boil. Using a large ladle, pour the boiling liquid over the shrimp and onions. Let stand until cool enough to handle, then refrigerate for at least 48 hours. Keep refrigerated and use within a week. Serve as a snack or hors d'oeuvres, perhaps with saltines and beer. Leftovers can be used in salads.

FRIED SHRIMP CHIPS

This cracker is made from fresh shrimp, tapioca, and egg white. Raw chips, which must be fried before serving, are available in some Asian markets. They're eaten alone or with appetizers. I like them with a huge shrimp salad for lunch, or with beer at any time.

4 ounces raw shrimp chips
peanut oil

Pour 1 inch of peanut oil into a shallow 8-inch pan or skillet. Heat until quite hot, then reduce the heat to medium. Carefully drop in two or three shrimp chips. Press them down with a wooden spoon or chopsticks, helping them expand into large crackers. (If the oil is too hot, the chips won't expand properly.) Remove and drain each chip, placing it on a brown bag or paper towels to drain. These can be eaten warm, or stored in a suitable container until needed. If stored in a vacuum bag, they will stay crunchy for weeks.

Salads

The recipe isn't really the key to a good shrimp salad. Having freshly cooked shrimp, preferably boiled, that are tender and juicy will make a good salad when served with only shredded lettuce and a little mayonnaise.

EASY SHRIMP SALAD

This basic recipe works as a salad served up on lettuce leaves, or as a stuffing for avocado or tomato halves. It can be made with leftover boiled shrimp, but it's best when made from scratch.

1½ pounds beheaded raw shrimp, medium (2 pounds heads-on shrimp)
2 ribs celery with tops, finely chopped
1 large hard-boiled chicken egg, finely chopped

2 tablespoons good mayonnaise
1 tablespoon sweet pickle relish
salt and pepper to taste
lettuce leaves
salted water

Boil the shrimp in salted water for 2 or 3 minutes, or until they turn nicely pink. Drain and shuck the shrimp. (If you want Shrimp Stock for another recipe, save the head and peelings. Proceed with the recipe on page 181.) Chill and chop the shrimp. Mix all the remaining ingredients except the lettuce leaves, adding salt and pepper to taste. Serve on lettuce leaves along with crackers or melba toast. Serve with Fried Shrimp Chips, page 153. Makes 4 to 6 salad servings.

SHRIMP AND AVOCADO SALAD

The success of this dish depends largely on having very ripe avocados. Although it works best as a side dish to a main meal, I can make a lunch of this salad, partly because avocados are so rich and filling. Don't cut back on the mayonnaise in this recipe; it goes nicely with avocado.

¾ **pound beheaded raw shrimp, medium or small (1 pound heads-on shrimp)**
2 **large avocados**
¼ **red bell pepper, finely chopped**
1 **green onion with top, finely chopped**

¾ **cup good mayonnaise (preferably homemade)**
salt and white pepper to taste
Hungarian paprika (for garnish)
lemon wedges (for garnish)
water

Boil the shrimp in salted water for 3 or 4 minutes, or until they turn pink. Peel, devein, and chop the shrimp with a chef's knife or food mill. (If you use an electric device for chopping, be careful that you don't puree them.) Mix the mayonnaise, shrimp, onion, bell pepper, salt, and white pepper. Set aside. Cut the avocados in half lengthwise, remove the pits, and sprinkle lightly with salt. Stuff each avocado half with the shrimp mixture. Sprinkle lightly with paprika. Serve on a small plate, along with lemon wedges and perhaps a few sprigs of fresh parsley from your herb garden. Feeds 2 or 4.

SHRIMP RÉMOULADE

This is a very popular salad in New Orleans, where it's made with either a white mayonnaise (as in this recipe) or with a mixture of brown prepared mustard and white mayonnaise. There hundreds of sauce recipes, but the basic salad is pretty much the same, made with peeled boiled shrimp and served up on a bed of lettuce

1½ pounds beheaded raw
   shrimp, large (2 pounds
   heads-on shrimp)
1 cup good mayonnaise
juice of ½ lemon
¼ cup chopped fresh parsley
2 tablespoons dry sherry or
   vermouth
2 tablespoons white wine
   vinegar
2 tablespoons capers

1 tablespoon minced
   green onion
½ tablespoon minced
   fresh garlic
½ teaspoon dry mustard
½ teaspoon sugar
⅛ teaspoon Tabasco sauce
salt to taste
lettuce
water

Boil the shrimp in water for 2 or 3 minutes. Drain, cool, and shuck the shrimp. (If you want stock for another recipe, put the heads, tails, and peelings back into the water and proceed with the recipe on page 181.) Chill the shrimp. In a bowl, mix the rest of the ingredients except the lettuce. Mix in the chilled shrimp. Chill for 2 hours or longer. Serve on a bed of lettuce, either on a large platter or on individual salad plates. Feeds 3 or 4 for lunch, or more as an appetizer for a fried-shrimp dinner.

Sandwiches and Wrap-Arounds

Shrimp aren't often considered as sandwich stuff, but be sure to try these recipes.

SHRIMP FAJITAS

Shrimp that have been sautéed in butter for 2 or 3 minutes, perhaps with a little lemon juice, make excellent fajitas. Grilled shrimp also work, as do those cooked in a grilling machine. It's best, always, to serve the tortillas, cooked shrimp, and go-withs separately, letting everyone make their own.

dressed raw shrimp, cut in half lengthwise	salt and pepper
olive oil	fresh 7-inch flour tortillas
lemon juice	chunky salsa
	a selection of toppings

Place several fresh tortillas in aluminum foil, seal, and warm them in the oven or over the grill. Keep them warm while you prepare the shrimp. Heat the olive oil in a skillet over high heat, using just enough oil to cover the bottom. Cook the shrimp for a minute, turn, and cook for another minute. Ideally, the high heat will cook through the shrimp halves quickly and impart a nice color, pink and brown. Sprinkle with a little lemon juice, salt, and pepper. Remove from the heat. Have ready a good salsa or, better, an assortment of salsa ingredients and condiments, each in separate bowls, along with plenty of shredded lettuce. The complete assortment would include chopped onions, chopped fresh tomatoes, guacamole, shredded cheeses, salt, and freshly ground black pepper. When the shrimp are ready, slice them in half and put them on a heated cast-iron serving griddle (preferably with a wicker trivet). Unwrap the tortillas. Top each one with shrimp and salsa, along with individual choice of condiments. Servings? If the fajitas are for the main meal, I'll take at least 2. Maybe 3 or 4, depending on how fat they are. In any case, I allow at least ¼ pound of dressed shrimp per person.

SHRIMP SUBS

There are now thousands of variations on this popular sandwich, made with a small loaf of French or Italian bread or a "hoagie" loaf. Here's my approach to a shrimp sub. I don't offer exact measures for the ingredients, but generally I allow ¼ pound of shrimp per sub.

shrimp, fully dressed, small to medium	**mayonnaise or Rémoulade Sauce (see page 179)**
hoagie rolls	**shredded lettuce**
cooking oil	**chopped or sliced tomatoes**
flour	**minced onion (optional)**
melted butter	**salt and freshly ground black pepper**

Preheat the oven to 400 degrees and rig for deep frying. Cut off the top of each hoagie and hollow it considerably, making way for a generous portion of fried shrimp. Brush the insides of the hoagies with melted butter. Put the loaves into the center of the oven for about 5 minutes. While you're waiting, sprinkle the shrimp lightly with salt, shake in a bag of flour, and deep fry until nicely browned. Do not overcook. Smear some mayonnaise or Rémoulade Sauce into the hoagies and partly fill with shrimp. Sprinkle on some shredded lettuce, minced onion (if wanted), and chopped tomato, along with some salt and freshly ground black pepper. Replace the tops and serve hot. With fries and a suitable drink, these make a very good lunch.

Variation: Save the tops for bread crumbs or for sopping bread. Sprinkle each hoagie with shredded mozzarella. Broil until the cheese is bubbly. Serve open faced.

SHRIMP EGG ROLLS

These days egg roll skins can be purchased from the supermarket, which makes this recipe easier. (If you prefer to make your own skins, have at it.) A 1-pound package of supermarket skins will make about 18 egg rolls. You'll need two packages for this recipe. That's a lot of egg rolls, I'll admit, but the measures can be cut in half. Still, since you've got to boil shrimp and heat up lots of oil for deep frying, why not make enough to freeze? These can be quickly thawed and heated in a microwave, making handy snacks. I'll take 2 or 3 for a light lunch.

It's best to use a large deep fryer with peanut oil heated to 350 to 375 degrees. This temperature will seal the outside of the egg rolls, keeping them from becoming too greasy.

2¼ pounds beheaded raw shrimp, medium (3 pounds heads-on shrimp)
1 pound bacon
2 medium onions
2 stalks celery with green tops
2 cups bok choy, cut into matchsticks
1 cup chopped fresh sunchokes (Jerusalem artichokes) or canned water chestnuts
1 red bell pepper, cut into matchsticks

1 green bell pepper, cut into matchsticks
3 chicken eggs
2 tablespoons soy sauce
1 tablespoon chopped fresh cilantro (with roots, if available)
1 teaspoon grated fresh gingerroot
about 3 dozen egg roll skins
peanut oil for deep frying
water

1. Boil the shrimp in water for 2 or 3 minutes, or until they turn pink and shuck easily. Plunge the shrimp into cold water. Drain and shuck the shrimp, saving the heads, tails, and peelings for stock (page 181) if wanted. Grind the shrimp in a food mill, or mince finely.

2. Rig for deep frying at 375 degrees. In a skillet, fry the bacon until it's crisp. Drain, crumble, and set aside.

3. Mix the ginger with the soy sauce in a large bowl. Add the peppers, celery, bok choy, chopped cilantro, onion, and sunchokes. Stir in the eggs. Add the shrimp, mixing well. Put about 1 tablespoon of the mixture on each egg roll skin. Fold the skins (following the directions on the package), roll, and seal with a little water.

4. Deep fry a few rolls at a time until they're slightly browned. Drain. Serve with mustard and honey sauce, or with a dipping sauce of your choice.

If you want to freeze some of these, simply wrap them individually in microwavable plastic wrap. When you're ready to snack, punch a hole in the plastic wrap and heat them in a microwave for a minute or two.

Raw Shrimp

Some people eat raw shrimp—which, of course, should be very, very fresh. In fact, the process should start with live shrimp that are beheaded, peeled, and consumed on the spot. Often, they're dipped into fresh seawater instead of a sauce, or perhaps seasoned with a drop or two of lemon juice.

The Japanese take this a step farther, trying to eat the shrimp while it's still kicking. This ritual usually takes place at a bar at which the attendant hands the diner the wiggling shrimp by the tail. The diner quickly dips the shrimp into a sauce and eats it at the bar, claiming that the wiggle adds to the flavor. Live shrimp for this treat are very expensive, and a special trade has developed to deliver them to the Japanese market.

SHRIMP SEVICHE

Here's a wonderful dish, but it must be made with very fresh shrimp. Note that the shrimp are not cooked, although some people say that the lime juice "cooks" them. They make a wonderful appetizer or first course, served up like a salad.

¾ pound beheaded shrimp, small or medium (1 pound heads-on raw shrimp)
juice of 4 limes or lemons
2 tablespoons finely chopped onion
1 tablespoon finely chopped green bell pepper

1 tablespoon finely chopped red bell pepper
1 tablespoon finely chopped fresh parsley
3 tablespoons olive oil
salt and black pepper

Shell the shrimp, put them into a nonmetallic bowl, and cover them with lime juice. Refrigerate for 2 hours, stirring once or twice. Drain the shrimp. In a serving bowl, mix the shrimp, onions, peppers, parsley, olive oil, salt, and pepper. Serve with crackers or bread thins. Makes 4 or more appetizer servings.

15

Dried Shrimp and Pastes

Our older cookbooks didn't offer many recipes for fresh shrimp, simply because they weren't widely available. Before canning was invented, the pickings were pretty much limited to dried shrimp, and Chinese and Philippine immigrants developed a thriving industry along the Louisiana and Texas Gulf Coasts. They actually dried the shrimp on platforms built on stilts out into the water, where the breeze and sun did the work. Some of these platforms were so clustered that they were called Manila Village.

The inventions of modern canning, mechanical refrigeration, and quick freezing gave us more and more fresh shrimp for the table. At the same time, our cookery lost the intense flavor of dried shrimp, which in some parts of the world is considered a seasoning or flavoring, available commercially in powdered or paste form. Indeed, dried shrimp are important to the cuisine of some lands, such as Burma. According to *The Burmese Kitchen*, by Copeland Marks, "A trip through Scott's

Market in Rangoon, the great central market of the city, is an eye opener. Mounds of dried shrimps in various sizes and shades of pink/orange greet eager buyers. They are an indispensable flavoring in soups and salads."

Moreover, making sauces and pastes from dried shrimp is a very old practice. The ancient Romans were fond of a sauce called garnum, usually made from fermented salted fish—and some of the best was made with salted shrimp. In modern times a salty paste has been made from tiny shrimp called doods, taken from a most unlikely source—salt ponds in the northern fringes of the Sahara Desert. I may have eaten some once, in Oran.

Fortunately for gourmets, shrimp are still dried in quantity today in Mexico, China, Brazil, and other parts of the world, usually for local consumption. In the United States they are available mostly in Asian markets. Usually these are tiny shrimp, but times change and I expect to see a wider selection in the future.

Here's my take on the current market forms.

DRIED SHRIMP

These are usually small Asian shrimp marketed in small packages, at least in this country at this time. They're available by mail order and in large ethnic shops. Clearly, America has a long way to go to catch up to Burma and other parts of the world on the use of dried shrimp—and other dried seafoods, such as squid and jellyfish.

SHRIMP POWDER

This can be purchased in Asian markets, or you can make your own simply by grinding dried shrimp with a mortar and pestle.

SHRIMP PASTE

This preparation can be purchased in tubes or jars in Asian markets. It should be refrigerated after opening. In a pinch you can make do by mashing some dried shrimp in a little peanut oil.

SHRIMP SAUCE

This condiment is available commercially in some Asian markets. In Vietnam, where it's called mam ruoc (with some tricky accent marks), it's often added to soups.

If you dry your own shrimp, start with small ones, beheaded. Use plenty of salt, which will help draw the moisture from the shrimp and discourage the growth of bacteria. Put these in the sun to dry, preferably with the help of a good sea breeze. After the shrimp are dried, the shells can be removed easily because the meat of the shrimp shrinks. It's best to seal dried shrimp in airtight containers and store them in a cool place. The modern kitchen dehydrators and vacuum-pack systems make drying and storing shrimp easier than ever before. It's best to follow the manufacturer's instructions.

Be sure to try these recipes for dried shrimp.

BALACHAUNG

The Burmese make several sauces with shrimp paste and dried shrimp powder. This one has been adapted from *Dining with Headhunters*, by Richard Sterling. Several others can be found in *The Burmese Kitchen*, by Copeland Marks, and in *The Hot Sauce Bible*, by Dave DeWitt and Chuck Evans. The chili pepper used in this recipe should be medium hot, such as the serrano; use hotter peppers if you want a hotter sauce.

½ pound coarsely ground
   dried shrimp
1 teaspoon shrimp paste
2 cups peanut oil
½ cup vinegar

4 small onions, thinly sliced
20 cloves garlic, sliced
1 fresh medium-hot red chili
   pepper, seeded and chopped
2 teaspoons salt

1. Mix the shrimp paste, vinegar, chili pepper, and salt. Set aside.

2. Heat the peanut oil in a skillet and sauté the onion for about 5 minutes. Remove with a slotted spoon and set aside. Sauté the garlic for 3 minutes. Remove with a slotted spoon and set aside.

3. Pour off part of the oil, leaving approximately 1 cup in the skillet. Fry the shrimp powder for 5 minutes. Add the onions and garlic; fry until they're crisp. Remove the skillet from the heat and let it cool. Stir in the vinegar mixture.

4. Put the sauce into a serving container and use as a table condiment. Serve over rice dishes or over plain rice. My dog Nosher likes a little over her Gravy Train.

DRIED SHRIMP SOUP

This easy dish is from Mexico, where small shrimp are dried on a large scale along some of the coastal areas. If you must, substitute 1 pound of fresh shrimp.

½ pound dried shrimp, ground
1 chicken breast, boned and
   ground
1 quart chicken stock (or 4 cups
   hot water with 4 bouillon cubes)

4 ripe tomatoes, peeled,
   seeded, and diced
½ cup minced onion
1 tablespoon minced fresh
   cilantro with roots

¼ cup butter

¼ cup almonds, peeled and
  ground

salt and pepper

lime quarters (optional)

Melt the butter in a saucepan. Sauté the onion and cilantro for a few minutes, then stir in the ground almonds with a wooden spoon. Add the chicken, chicken stock, and tomatoes. Add the shrimp, along with a little salt and pepper to taste. Simmer for 20 minutes. Serve hot in soup bowls, along with rolled tortillas and lime wedges for those who want to squeeze a little juice into the soup.

OSE OJI

Here's an unusual peanut butter from West Africa, according to *Best of Regional African Cooking,* by Harva Hachten. Flavored with either dried shrimp or dried crawfish, it's traditionally served with kola nuts. I like it on saltines. Also try Ose Oji with Fried Shrimp Chips (page 153).

2 cups roasted shelled peanuts

1 teaspoon ground dried shrimp

¼ teaspoon cayenne pepper

salt

oil, if needed

Mix the peanuts, ground shrimp, salt to taste, and cayenne. Process in a food mill or blender, adding a little oil if needed to make a peanut butter. Leave it a little chunky if you like it that way.

BALI SEAFOOD PASTE

This spicy paste is used with many fish and seafood dishes in Bali. It calls for salam leaves, which can be omitted. The tamarind pulp is essential and is available from Asian markets and by mail order. Turmeric root (which looks like ginger) may or may not be readily available, but turmeric powder can be substituted. Shrimp paste—an essential ingredient, strong and full of flavor—is available in Asian markets. The chili peppers should be only medium hot, as is the case with most large chili peppers.

15 shallots, chopped

10 large red chili peppers, seeded and chopped

6 cloves garlic, chopped

4 inches fresh gingerroot, chopped

4 inches fresh turmeric root, chopped, or 4 teaspoons powdered dried turmeric

1 medium tomato, peeled and chopped

10 candlenuts (or 6 Brazil nuts)

¼ cup cooking oil

3 tablespoons tamarind pulp

2 stalks lemongrass

1 teaspoon dried shrimp paste

2 salam leaves (optional)

Using a food mill, coarsely grind and thoroughly mix all the ingredients except the lemongrass, oil, tamarind, and salam leaves. In a skillet, heat the oil. Bruise the lemongrass and add it to the skillet, along with the salam leaves and the contents of the food mill. Sauté for 5 minutes, stirring as you go. Stir in the tamarind pulp and cool. Use as needed in seafood recipes.

BRAZILIAN SHRIMP SAUCE

This sauce, hot and strong, is served over bland foods. Make it with fresh malagueta chili peppers if available, or substitute Tabasco or other hot peppers of your choice—but be careful with the habanero fireballs.

6 large or jumbo shrimp,   1 medium to large onion, minced
   cooked, shucked, and   ¼ cup peanut oil
   minced   1 tablespoon fresh cilantro
5 fresh malagueta peppers,   with roots, minced
   or a substitute (see above)   salt to taste

Put the peppers, onion, cilantro, and shrimp in a mortar and
mash with a pestle, adding a little salt. Heat the oil in a small
pan. Sauté the shrimp paste for 10 minutes, stirring with a
wooden spoon. Serve with vegetable fritters or bland foods.

   Note: You can also make this with dried shrimp, soaking
them in water before grinding. Omit the salt.

A. D.'S FUSION PIZZA

We are seeing more and more about "fusion" cuisine these days,
and usually the recipes and their lists of ingredients are so long
it's hard to tell what tastes like what. Here's a fusion recipe of
my own doing—one of my personal fast-food favorites—that
doesn't require 36 ingredients or measurements thereof.

8-inch fresh flour tortillas   sharp cheddar cheese, shredded
tomato salsa (hot or mild,   dried shrimp, powdered
   as you like it)   or grated

Preheat the broiler. Spread some salsa onto each tortilla.
Sprinkle with shredded cheese and dried shrimp to taste. Broil
until the cheese bubbles and starts to turn brown. Enjoy, along
with a good Mexican beer.

   Note: I also use dried fish roe in this recipe instead of
shrimp. To dry fresh roe, simply sprinkle them heavily with salt
and leave them in a well-ventilated place. Repeat every day until
the water stops dripping out.

16

Shrimp Sauces, Stocks, and Go-Withs

A good many commercial sauces complement shrimp, or were formulated especially for eating with shrimp and seafood. Others are convenient for use in recipes, and sometimes for concocting other sauces. The most obvious of these include mayonnaise, ketchup, Worcestershire, soy sauce, mustard, and so on. Also, we are seeing more and more sauces from around the world on supermarket shelves, such as Asian fish sauce.

Sauces especially for shrimp and seafood include a few commercial rémoulade mixes, tartar sauces, and so on, along with regional favorites, which can sometimes be hard to find in nationwide markets. Gourmet catalogs that specialize in regional cooking may be the best source for the sauce buff, along with similar sites on the Internet. A recent Gazin's Cajun Creole Cuisine catalog, for example, contains two rémoulade sauces, one billed as Shrimp Arnaud Sauce, along with recipe-specific sauces such as Shrimp Scampi Sauce, Shrimp Mosca Mix,

"Barbecued" Shrimp Mix, and, of course, Shrimp Creole Mix. Hot red sauces, with the widely available Tabasco topping the list, are just too numerous to name. Some of these, often billed as Louisiana Hot Sauce, are made with red cayenne peppers. We also have green hot sauces, garlic hot sauces, bourbon hot sauces, voodoo hot sauces, and so on, and so on.

Spice mixes and blends are more readily available these days than sauces and are even more numerous in the gourmet catalogs. The Cajuns are professional spice mixers, offering us hundreds of blends of what I call Cajun Dust (see the recipe on page 180). Many of these are formulated for seafood and sometimes, the Cajuns say, especially for shrimp. Most of these mixes are packaged in a plastic or tin shake box. Some of the mixes are billed as seasoning or seasoning salts. These often have SEAFOOD or perhaps something like CHESAPEAKE BAY printed on the label, but some have a wider application. One of my favorites is lemon-pepper seasoning salt, which I find especially useful for sprinkling on grilled or broiled shrimp during the last few minutes of cooking.

In addition to dusts, we have various whole-spice mixes, similar to pickling spices. Some, billed as crab boil or shrimp boil, are packaged in small cloth bags. These can be put into the water for the boil and easily removed, without getting flecks of spices on the shrimp. Neat. But they aren't foolproof because a good deal of how much flavor is imparted to the shrimp depends on how long the spices steep in the liquid and on how long the shrimp are left in the spiced water, as I discussed at length in chapter 2.

Personally, I think the cook lucky enough to have fresh shrimp ought to pay more attention to cooking detail than to magic spice mixes (which have a way of running out when you need them most), and to good basic, readily available ingredients. Here's my take.

BLACK PEPPER AND PEPPERCORNS

For flavor and aroma, freshly ground black pepper is always better than boxed. An electric spice mill is good to have if you need lots of pepper, but most of us can get by with a hand-turned mill suitable for kitchen and table. It's best to grind only as much pepper as you need, simply because the whole peppercorns store better than does the ground pepper. Remember to put the pepper mill on the table.

SALT

By far the most important single seasoning in the kitchen. Sea salt is better than regular table salt. It has a more intense taste, containing traces of all the natural minerals of the sea. Coarse salt works fine for boiling and can be used in salt mills for table use. So after you buy a matching set of pepper and salt mills, you can throw out the spice rack. Almost.

BAY LEAVES

I like to put a bay leaf or two in dishes that are to be cooked uncovered in a liquid for a long while. The aroma fills the house and makes everybody hungry. It's best to fish the leaves out of such dishes as gumbo before serving.

HERBS

I lean toward fresh herbs whenever possible, but dried will work in most recipes if the measure is cut in half.

BUTTER

Real butter almost always works better in recipes than margarine. For skillet recipes cooked over high heat, butter tends to burn unless it's clarified. To clarify it, heat some butter in a saucepan for a few minutes. Note that some of the impurities will sink to the bottom and others will rise to the top. Skim off the top, then pour the clarified butter out of the pan carefully, leaving the impurities in the bottom.

OLIVE OIL

Use extra-virgin olive oil for most recipes. For deep frying, buy olive oil by the gallon. It can be strained and used again and again, although some books tell you to throw it out after the first use.

LEMON OR LIME JUICE

Use only freshly squeezed lemon juice or lime juice, if possible. Canned juice just isn't the same.

In any case, the best sauces for shrimp are made in the kitchen, using fresh ingredients. Usually, these sauces are quite simple to make.

BUTTER AND LEMON SAUCE

This plain dipping sauce is hard to beat with hot boiled shrimp, and for use as a basting sauce for grilled or broiled shrimp. It doesn't work too well for cold shrimp because the butter tends to solidify.

melted butter
freshly squeezed lemon juice
salt, if needed

Melt the butter in a saucepan and stir in the lemon juice, using about half and half—or to taste, such as 2 parts butter to 1 part lemon juice. I like a little salt in mine, especially if the butter is unsalted. Serve warm with boiled or steamed shrimp, providing individual dipping cups for each eater.

Notes: Substitute freshly squeezed lime juice if you have it at hand. Also note that butter sauces should not be served chilled or with chilled shrimp.

LADOLEMONO

This classic Greek sauce is made fresh for each meal. Try it over fried or grilled shrimp.

½ cup extra-virgin olive oil
¼ cup freshly squeezed
  lemon juice

salt and pepper to taste
chopped fresh parsley
  to taste (optional)

Whisk together the olive oil and lemon juice, adding a little salt, pepper, and chopped parsley (if you wish) to taste. Serve immediately at room temperature.

COCKTAIL SAUCE

Chilled shrimp (usually boiled or steamed) are often dipped into a red sauce, usually made by simply combining ketchup with prepared horseradish. I like some lemon juice in mine—and a few drops of Tabasco.

1 cup ketchup
3 tablespoons freshly
  squeezed lemon juice

2 tablespoons prepared mild
  horseradish sauce
6 drops Tabasco sauce (or to taste)

Mix all the ingredients well and pour into a serving bowl. Serve with chilled boiled or steamed shrimp.

TARTAR SAUCE FOR SHRIMP

There are more complex recipes for tartar sauce, but this one is really hard to beat.

1 cup good mayonnaise	1 clove garlic, minced
2 tablespoons finely chopped salad pickles	1 tablespoon minced fresh parsley or cilantro
2 tablespoons minced green onions with tops	1 teaspoon prepared yellow mustard
1 tablespoon minced red bell pepper	½ teaspoon prepared horseradish

Mix all ingredients in a serving container. Refrigerate for an hour before using. Serve as a condiment with fried shrimp.

TARATOR SAUCE

Not to be confused with Tartar Sauce (previous recipe), this garlic sauce from the Middle East goes with fried as well as broiled shrimp.

½ cup olive oil	3 to 6 cloves garlic
¼ cup freshly squeezed lemon juice	salt to taste

Mash the garlic with mortar and pestle. Add the salt. Work in about half the olive oil and let the sauce sit for 20 minutes. Then add the rest of the olive oil and the lemon juice, mixing well. Use as a sauce or a dip.

DILL SAUCE

This sauce goes with many fish and shellfish recipes. I like it with boiled jumbo shrimp.

1 cup sour cream
1½ tablespoons freshly
    squeezed lemon juice

1 teaspoon chopped fresh
    dill weed
sea salt to taste

Mix all the ingredients in a serving bowl. Refrigerate until needed. Serve cold, spooning a little over large cooked shrimp.

NUOC CHAM

Vietnamese or Thai fish sauce is essential to this condiment. Called Nuoc Cham (with some tricky accent marks over the vowels), it's served with just about every meal in Vietnam, north or south, and is best prepared fresh for each meal with the aid of a mortar and pestle. It goes nicely with fried seafood. I normally use a fresh cayenne pepper for the recipe, but any fresh red chili will do if it's seeded. Be sure to try this one.

2 tablespoons Vietnamese or
    Thai fish sauce
2 teaspoons brown sugar
1 clove garlic

½ hot red chili pepper,
    fresh or to taste
⅛ lime (wedge)
water to taste

Seed and mince the pepper, carefully removing the inner pith as well as the seeds. Peel and mince the garlic. Put the pepper and garlic into a mortar, along with the sugar. Grind into a paste. Squeeze the juice of the lime into the mortar, then remove the pulp with a baby spoon or small knife and work it into the mixture with the pestle. Add the fish sauce and a little water, blending well. Put the sauce into a small bowl and put it on the table, warning your guests to use it sparingly and infrequently, lest they become addicts.

PINK DIP

This dipping sauce works best with chilled shrimp that have been boiled or steamed.

½ cup good mayonnaise
½ cup prepared chili sauce
1 tablespoon tarragon
   vinegar

¾ teaspoon shrimp paste
   or anchovy paste
Tabasco sauce to taste (4 or
   5 drops will usually do)

Mix all the ingredients in a serving bowl and chill. This can be put into a cocktail glass with tails-on boiled shrimp arranged around the rim.

GREEN PEPPERCORN SAUCE

This sauce goes nicely with grilled or smoked shrimp. Note that the green peppercorns should be packed in water.

8 ounces sour cream
2 tablespoons green peppercorns
fine sea salt to taste

Crush the green peppercorns with mortar and pestle. Transfer to a small serving bowl, then mix in the salt and sour cream. Chill until needed.

A. D.'S EASY TEMPURA DIP

I like this sauce with tempura or other fried shrimp. It should be used sparingly as a dip. In other words, touch just the end of shrimp into the dip instead of dunking it halfway.

½ cup prepared mustard
¼ cup soy sauce
1 tablespoon honey

Mix all the ingredients at room temperature. Serve in small dipping bowls as a condiment with tempura or similar fried shrimp with a heavy batter.

RÉMOULADE SAUCE

This sauce goes nicely with boiled or steamed shrimp, either as a dip, with Shrimp Subs (page 158), or as a topping for Shrimp Rémoulade salad (page 156), which see. It doesn't go nicely with the highly spiced Cajun boils, however.

1 cup good mayonnaise (preferably homemade)
2 tablespoons minced green onion with tops
1 tablespoon minced capers
1 tablespoon minced fresh parsley
1 tablespoon minced red bell pepper
1 tablespoon minced anchovies
1 teaspoon dry mustard
½ teaspoon prepared horseradish
½ tablespoon minced fresh tarragon
¼ teaspoon white pepper

Put the mayonnaise into a bowl, then slowly stir in the rest of the ingredients until well mixed. Do not use an electric beater or otherwise blend lots of air into the sauce. It should be thick, smooth, and heavy. Refrigerate the sauce and serve cold.

Note: Every chef in New Orleans, and just about every cook in the state of Louisiana, has his own version of this sauce. In general, a Creole or Cajun rémoulade will have a brownish color, owing to the addition to lots of prepared Dijon-type mustard.

CAJUN DUST

This recipe is a basic seasoning mix for shellfish, containing a minimum of ingredients. Professional Cajuns will want to increase the recipe, using at least 25 ingredients. Suit yourself.

½ cup sea salt, finely ground

¼ cup ground red cayenne pepper

2 tablespoons Hungarian paprika

1 tablespoon freshly fine-ground black pepper

1 tablespoon onion powder

1 tablespoon garlic powder

1 tablespoon Accent

Thoroughly mix all the ingredients. Store in an airtight jar in a cool place until needed. It can be used as a rub for fish and meat. I use it as a sprinkle-on seasoning for shrimp cooked and served in the shell, to be shucked at the table. The seasoning gets on the fingers and shrimp during the peeling.

Shrimp Stocks

Shrimp peelings and heads make an excellent stock that can be used in recipes that call for fish stock, clam broth, or, sometimes, chicken stock. The peelings alone will work, but the heads make a richer stock.

The heads, tails, and peelings from boiled shrimp can be used, but usually the boil will contain quite a bit of salt or spices. My personal preference is to use shrimp that will be peeled before serving. The stock can be made from the water in which they were boiled (cutting back on the salt) or from the fresh heads and peelings in case the shrimp are to be fried or otherwise shucked before they reach the table.

Some of the recipes for this book call for Shrimp Stock. If you don't have this on hand and don't have the makings, you can substitute fish stock or sometimes even chicken stock.

STOCK FROM HEADS AND PEELINGS

The measures in this recipe aren't exact, and should be adjusted for the amount of shrimp peelings you have. I recommend making the stock rather strong. It can be refrigerated and diluted with water to taste.

heads and peelings from
  4 pounds shrimp
2 tablespoons olive oil
2 ribs celery with tops, chopped
1 medium to large onion,
  chopped
3 cloves garlic, chopped

1 tablespoon chopped
  fresh parsley
4 allspice berries
2 bay leaves
salt and freshly ground
  black pepper
6 cups water

Heat the oil in a saucepan. Add the shrimp heads and peelings. Cook over medium-high heat, tossing with a wooden spoon, for several minutes, until the heads turn pink. Add the rest of the ingredients, bring to a boil, reduce the heat, cover, and simmer for 30 minutes, or until the liquid thickens to your taste. Strain the stock, discarding the solids. Store in jars in the refrigerator until needed. It will keep for several days. Freeze it for longer storage.

STOCK FROM THE BOIL

Boil the shrimp for 2 or 3 minutes. Drain and shuck them, putting the heads and peelings back into the pot. (Sometimes the tails will be left on the shrimp for use as a handle.) Add standard stock ingredients (such as celery and onions), bring to a boil, and cook until the liquid is reduced by half. Strain and refrigerate until needed.

Note: Remember that highly salted water for the boil will make a salty stock. Either cut back on the salt in the water or reduce the salt in recipes calling for the finished stock.

Breads for Shrimp

The *Bubba Gump Shrimp Co. Cookbook* ends with a chapter called "Goes Real Good With," and the chapter itself ends with two recipes for cornbread: one for a cracklin' bread and another called Southern Hush Puppies, containing chicken eggs, cheddar cheese, jalapeño peppers, chopped onion, milk, lots of cream-style corn, and self-rising flour mixed with self-rising cornmeal, if you can believe all that. I may get kicked out of the South and might even get my name struck from the *Southern Living* mailing list, but I have to say that fried cornbread really doesn't go with shrimp. Of course, I'll eat really good cracklin' bread (if it's made with skinless cracklings and fresh stone-ground white cornmeal) at any time with anything, but it really isn't the best choice for shrimp.

A chewy French- or Italian-type loaf bread, San Francisco sourdough, or at least a garlic-flavored white bread, served hot, simply goes better with boiled shrimp and with most shrimp dishes. An exception calling for fried cornbread might be a fried seafood platter, where fried shrimp is served along with fried fish, fried oysters, and so on, making for lots of fried stuff.

Rice for Shrimp

A good many shrimp dishes call for rice. Any good recipe will do—but the rice should not be sticky, as a rule. Use a good long-grain rice and cook it to perfection, so that each grain stands out from its fellows. My choice, for shrimp, is a good basmati rice, as cooked in the recipe below. Almost always I prefer a white rice, although brown is the more healthy choice. Often shrimp are served on a pilaf, usually white rice cooked with stock and a saffronlike coloring. For additional color, I like to add some roasted red pepper, finely chopped. I also like to serve rice combined half and half with another grain or bean—perhaps lentils, which require about the same amount of cooking time, or shiny black beans, which should be cooked separately and mixed with rice after being well drained. Canned black beans, drained and rinsed, will do.

BASMATI RICE

Most basmati rice is purchased in fancy boxes or packages, along with a recipe or cooking directions. You might also try this recipe.

1 cup basmati rice
water
salt to taste

Rinse the rice under running water for several minutes, until the water runs clean. Rinse again and soak the rice in water for 30 minutes. Drain. Heat the rice in 4 quarts of water, adding a little salt. Boil vigorously for 5 minutes. Drain and gently fluff the rice with a fork, scraping it off the top.

Salad

A good vegetable or fruit salad and a loaf of bread are all you need with most shrimp dishes to make a complete meal. Try your favorite tossed or chef's salad, or use the recipe below if you have fresh tomatoes.

A. D.'S TOMATO SALAD

I eat this salad often if I have or can beg or steal vine-ripened tomatoes from my neighbors. Some cooks seed their tomatoes before making a salad, but I don't bother with this step. Suit yourself.

4 large ripe tomatoes,
   chopped
1 large white onion, preferably
   Vidalia, chopped
¼ cup chopped fresh parsley,
   chopped
¼ cup extra-virgin olive oil

juice of 2 lemons
1 teaspoon red wine vinegar
salt and freshly ground
   black pepper to taste
crisply fried bacon or
   cracklings, crumbled
(optional)

Toss all the ingredients except the bacon in a large wooden bowl. Put the bowl on the table next to a pile of boiled or fried shrimp, letting everybody put some into salad bowls or onto their plates. Serve the crumbled bacon in a small bowl for those who want to sprinkle a little onto the salad. Serves 2 or more.

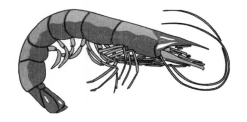

Index